PRAYING MARK

John Reilly SJ

PRAYING MARK

sp

St Paul Publications

ENGLISH TRANSLATION OF THE GOSPEL OF MARK
The Gospel of Mark is from the *New Revised Standard Version Bible*, copyright 1989 by the Division of Christian Education of the National Council of the Churches of Christ in the USA. Used by permission.

PRAYING MARK

First published, September 1992

National Library of Australia
Cataloguing-in-Publication data:
Reilly, John, 1928-
Praying Mark
ISBN 0 949080 95 0
1. Bible. N.T. Mark — Commentaries. 2. Prayer. I. Title.
226.3077

Cover illustration: Christmas stamp design reproduced with permission of Australia Post (George Hamori, 1973)
Cover design: Bruno Colombari ssp

Published by
ST PAUL PUBLICATIONS — Society of St Paul,
PO Box 230 — Homebush, NSW 2140

St Paul Publications is an activity of the Priests and Brothers of the Society of St Paul who proclaim the Gospel through the media of social communication

WITH GRATITUDE

*I would like to acknowledge
the help given to me
during the writing of this book
by different friends,
scholars and pray-ers,
who took time to read parts of it.*

FOREWORD

Reading the Gospel of Mark as a story is one thing. Researching its roots in history is another. Using it for prayer is still something more, consciously involving in some way the devout faith of a reader.

Praying Mark tries to combine 'exegesis' with what one might call 'eisegesis'. It attempts to balance reading Mark's meaning out of his text with reading a personal meaning into the text from the situation of one's own life. This is done here in the tradition of Ignatian spirituality, which has its roots in the spiritual or fuller sense of Scripture, sought by writers of the church from the first centuries of Christianity. If biblical scholarship and devout faith exist apart, both are losers.

When the understandings and experiences which people of the first century had of Jesus as the Christ during his lifetime and after his death, recorded creatively by Mark, begin also to be felt personally by us within the happenings of our lives today, the Gospel of Mark is being spiritually read.

Each episode in Mark's Gospel will be found on the left side of a page-opening, and on the right a brief commentary. The text of the Gospel is the New Revised Standard Version (1989), remarkable for its simplicity and clarity as well as its delicately inclusive language. The text is arranged by chapters and verses in the usual way, allowing for an easy reading of the entire Gospel. The commentary is systematically presented in seven major parts, each with a varying number of episodes.

Read a passage from Mark first, slowly and attentively. If already thoughts or feelings flow, stay with your own insights and emotions. The 'starters' may help. When the commentary is used, it is best read slowly and thoughtfully. This may lead one back to a further pondering of Mark's own words in his Gospel.

John Reilly, SJ

CONTENTS

9

According to Mark

This title was added only later in the early centuries of Christianity, identifying the author with John Mark of the New Testament, a companion of both Peter and Paul, it seems. Originally it was written anonymously.

It is the shortest of the four Gospels in the Bible and the only one of the four to be explicitly linked by its author to the gospel. It is generally understood to be the first of the four to be written, probably by a Jewish Christian author in Galilee or southern Syria after the Roman-Jewish war from 66-74. This was a time of great violence and bloodshed, at the height of which in the year 70 the Jerusalem temple was destroyed by the victorious Roman army.

The author was almost certainly not an eyewitness of the events he described. He skilfully selected some of the memories about Jesus and wrote them down creatively in a narrative with a definite purpose in view, which differs from that of the other Gospel authors, Matthew, Luke or John.

When he wrote, it is unlikely that the author intended a 'spiritual' interpretation to be read into his stories of Jesus, for his purpose was different. Yet once we have grasped his central message about the power of God breaking into the world in the person of Jesus and the increasing failure of the disciples to understand this, he surely would rejoice that Christians would seek and find in his stories their own life experiences of Christ. In different ways, Christians have done this with the stories in all the four Gospels since the early centuries of Christianity.

Starters

1. *A person called Mark is mentioned often in the New Testament. Look up some of these places: Col 4:10, Philem 24, 2 Tim 4:11, 1 Pet 5:13, Acts 12:12, 25, 13:5, 13, 15:37-39.*
2. *Compare the length of the Gospel of Mark with the lengths of the Gospels of Matthew, Luke and John.*

The Gospel according to Mark

Broadly speaking, we find in Mark what we look for. The author's concern was to present from his own perspective what the Christian community in which he lived, probably in Galilee or southern Syria, remembered about Jesus, and the inclusion of his Gospel by the church in the New Testament confirms that he did this authentically.

By reading Mark's Gospel reflectively we can find something of what Jesus historically said and did. Much more we find what the early church believed about Jesus. Above all, we find a Christian author's creative re-writing of the past life and death of Jesus in the light of his own present situation.

In addition to these three levels of reading, there is another. When anyone prayerfully brings to a personal reading of Mark's stories of Jesus the fabric and content of one's own life, there is created for the Gospel of Mark a kind of fourth dimension.

We could describe this as the spiritual dimension, an interior view through faith of the deeper meaning of the events of one's own life today when prayerfully pondered in the light of a Gospel. It is such a spiritual reading that the tradition of Ignatian spirituality always seeks in the narrative of a Gospel.

It greatly helps our approach to Mark's Gospel if we know that the author, whoever he was, was not trying to write a biography of Jesus as we understand it today. He presented his stories of Jesus as a creative form of the gospel, the good news from God!

The core of the gospel, 'god-spel' or 'good news', is about the power that God revealed in raising to a new life the same Jesus whom people killed on the cross. In this perspective Mark wrote to stir his readers to a more committed life as Christians and to encourage them in their difficulties.

I

JESUS INTRODUCED

Mark 1:1-13

Mark 1:1

1 The beginning of the good news of Jesus Christ, the Son of God.

Starters

1. *Mark alone of the four evangelists uses the word gospel or good news. Reflect a little on these passages: 1:1, 14, 15, 8:35, 10:29, 13:10, 14:9, and 16:15.*

2. *Look up some passages in the New Testament where Paul, who wrote before Mark, uses gospel or good news as a noun or a verb: 1 Thess 2:2, 4, 8, 9, 1 Cor 1:17, Rom 1:1-4, 9, 16-17.*

3. *The core of the gospel is witness to the crucifixion and raising of Jesus. Read some of the ways this is said in the Letters of Paul and the Acts of the Apostles: 1 Thess 1:5, 1 Cor 1:23-24, Rom 4:25, Acts 2:22-24, 32-33, 36, 3:13-15, 4:10, 5:30-32, 8:34-35, 10:37-41.*

4. *The word 'Christ', which is the same as 'Messiah', occurs seven times in Mark: 1:1, 8:29, 9:41, 12:35, 13:21, 14:61, 15:32.*

5. *Jesus is named the Son of God twice by God himself: Mark 1:11, 9:7, and on five other occasions: 1:1, 3:11, 5:7, 14:61, 15:39.*

I/1. Mark's title

In the first line Mark gives his title. He writes of Jesus as Christ and Son of God. 'Christ' is Greek for 'Messiah', a Hebrew word. It meant in ancient Israel a king, a priest, or sometimes a prophet, anointed by God with oil for a task, but especially an anointed one yet to come. Early Christians confessed Jesus to be the 'Christ', not just because he fulfilled Old Testament prophecies, but because he was raised to life by God for a task in the New Testament by a unique anointing, not with oil but with Holy Spirit.

Jesus was confessed as 'Son of God' by the first Christians because they believed he shared uniquely, like a son with a father, throughout his whole life, but especially by his resurrection in God's power to breathe the Holy Spirit into the world.

The centrepiece of Mark's Gospel is Peter's confession of Jesus as the 'Messiah' (8:29), and its climax is the Roman centurion's confession of Jesus as 'Son of God' (15:39).

When Mark called his work the 'beginning' of the gospel, was he simply saying that this first line (1:1) was the beginning of his story? Was he saying that the gospel began with the coming of John the Baptiser (1:2-8)? Or was he most likely saying that everything he wrote about Jesus (1:2—16:8) was the 'beginning' or foundation of the gospel which the church was sent to announce? Mark's challenge is by exposing the roots of the church's gospel in the historical events of the life and death of Jesus.

The gospel which the church proclaimed in the '30s, '40s, '50s and '60s of the first century was the power of God raising a crucified Jesus. Mark remarkably ended his Gospel where he probably did (16:8), with no resurrection stories. It appears he wanted to put firmly before his readers the way of opposition and misunderstanding which Jesus walked in his lifetime.

2 As it is written in the prophet Isaiah, 'See, I am sending my messenger ahead of you, who will prepare your way; 3 The voice of one crying out in the wilderness: "Prepare the way of the Lord, make his paths straight".'

4 John the baptiser appeared in the wilderness, proclaiming a baptism of repentance for the forgiveness of sins.

5 And people from the whole Judean countryside and all the people of Jerusalem were going out to him, and were baptised by him in the river Jordan, confessing their sins.

6 Now John was clothed with camel's hair, with a leather belt around his waist, and he ate locusts and wild honey.

7 He proclaimed, 'The one who is more powerful than I is coming after me; I am not worthy to stoop down and untie the thong of his sandals.

8 'I have baptised you with water; but he will baptise you with the Holy Spirit.'

Starters

1. *Try to feel within yourself some of the atmosphere around John as crowds flocked to hear him in the desert.*

2. *How much do I see myself turned towards God and prepared to welcome his coming into my life?*

I/2. The preaching of John

The prologue of Mark's Gospel (1:1-13) introduces Jesus as he really is. He does this first through John the baptiser, the last of the Old Testament prophets. Mark compares him with Elijah, God's messenger in the prophecy of Malachy (Mal 3:1), and with the desert prophet in Isaiah (Is 40:3). Like Elijah John wears a leather belt and eats a desert food of locusts and honey (2 Kings 1:8).

Physical going into the desert to hear John is of no use without an interior emptying of all self-righteousness and self-reliance. The baptism of conversion asked of all by John is more than repentance and turning from self-centredness. It must also be a turning towards God under the influence of his healing and creative action. Mark called it in Greek a baptism of 'metanoia'. 'Meta-noia' literally means 'other-mind', or a new attitude of God-centredness to replace self-centredness.

John was called the baptiser because he symbolised a way into the future by a baptism of conversion. His baptism in water symbolised dramatically a personal readiness of heart for a baptism with divine Spirit to be given by Jesus, the more powerful one coming after him.

To experience the gospel we must be people of the future. The whole of this opening passage fixes our vision on the future. We can be people of the future only if we experience a radical change of heart. We need to become persons filled with a deep desire for the good that comes from the future. Radical hope coming from interior conversion is the true way into the future.

God-centredness cannot be realised by human effort alone. We prepare ourselves for it as we wait for it to come as a gift. It comes by a baptism with the Holy Spirit brought by the one to whom Mark directs our gaze through the figure of John the baptiser.

Mark 1:9-11

⁹In those days Jesus came from Nazareth of Galilee and was baptised by John in the Jordan.

¹⁰And just as he was coming up out of the water, he saw the heavens torn apart and the Spirit descending like a dove on him.

¹¹And a voice came from heaven, 'You are my Son the Beloved; with you I am well pleased.'

Starters

1. *Reflect on why Jesus can mix so easily with the people coming to hear John.*

2. *Try to share something of the experience Jesus had of God at the river, expressed by the three symbols: the split sky, the dove, the voice.*

I/3. The baptism of Jesus

Here Mark has God himself introduce Jesus to his readers. Mark describes him simply as a man coming from Nazareth in Galilee, a place mentioned nowhere in the Old Testament. All that happened to Jesus before this is left to our imagination and devotion.

This event at the river is for Mark more significant. It allows us, as the readers of Mark, in our first meeting with Jesus to see him as the Messiah standing with his people and to know from the outset how God himself sees Jesus, as his own loved Son.

In Mark's Gospel, the split heavens, the dove and the voice after the baptism are more important than the baptism itself. The experience of these, in Mark's Gospel, is for Jesus only, and for us the readers to know.

The heavens or sky split open is God revealing himself a new awareness of God breaking into the human consciousness of Jesus and through him into the world. The dove expresses the love, the peace and the Spirit of God which surround Jesus.

The voice from the heavens describes Jesus as the faithful servant of the prophecy of Isaiah (Is 42:1), but says much more. It identifies Jesus as the Son of God, having an intimacy with God which can compare only with the special intimacy of life between parent and child.

Why would Jesus want to be baptised by John? Jesus never asked forgiveness for a sin of his own. His baptism by John could only have been a true expression of his deep longing to be totally centred on God. It was also a way of acknowledging John's work and showing human solidarity with all of us. Jesus was not just giving good example to others when he asked for John's baptism of conversion. His action could only have come from genuine interior feelings.

Mark 1:12-13

¹² *And the Spirit immediately drove him out into the wilderness.*

¹³ *He was in the wilderness forty days, tempted by Satan; and he was with the wild beasts; and the angels waited on him.*

Starters

1. *Ponder how the Holy Spirit, which comes to Jesus at the river, stirs in him the desire to confront Satan, the enemy of all that is human.*

2. *Consider Satan, the beasts, and the angels as symbols to express what Jesus experienced in the desert when he went to be tested by Satan.*

3. *Feel the tension between the Holy Spirit and the desert, both of which are prominent in all three episodes of the prologue (1:2-13).*

I/4. Jesus in the desert

Driven by God's Spirit, Jesus goes to the desert to confront Satan, the source of dehumanising evil. We are shown what the Messiah is sent to do, defeat Satan in his own territory.

In the Bible, the desert saw creation begin (Gen 2). It was the place of testing for the Israelites on their way to the promised land (Ex 32:8). It was the place of loneliness where the beasts lived. It was the home of evil powers, which the wild beasts symbolised. Satan, the prince of evil and opponent of God, lived there. Yet the desert is also the place where Moses spoke with God on the mountain for forty days (Ex 34:28), and the place where the prophet Elijah travelled for forty days to the holy mountain on the strength of the food given him by an angel (1 Kings 19:8).

Here we see the true identity of Jesus, one bringing divine power against Satan; one who can be with the beasts, symbols of suffering and violent persecution (Dan 7), like a new Adam controlling them; and one whom God strengthens by angels. In Jesus, God deals with evil and creates again.

The interior spiritual experience of Jesus in the desert is left for our devotion to discover. He was in the desert for forty days. Unlike the chosen people of God in the Old Testament, Jesus remains faithful.

Whatever happened to Jesus in the desert could be like a Satan, that is, temptations to oppose God and be unfaithful to the task God has given him. Or it could be like the beasts who ignore God, going their own violent ways. Or thirdly, it could be like the angels, helping Jesus to serve God faithfully and discern his role in God's plan. For us too life can provide its Satans opposing God, its beasts making us unmindful of God, and its angels helping us to serve God.

II

JESUS CALLS DISCIPLES

Mark 1:14 — 3:6

Mark 1:14-15

14 Now after John was arrested, Jesus came to Galilee, proclaiming the good news of God,

15 and saying, 'The time is fulfilled, and the kingdom of God has come near; repent, and believe in the good news.'

Starters

1. *Reflect for a while on the key words here, for they contain the substance and purpose of all the things Jesus said and did.*

2. *Try to get in touch with any desire you truly feel in yourself for the power of God to free from evil, which Jesus called the kingdom of God.*

II/1. Summary: the mission of Jesus

In the prologue of Mark's Gospel (1:1-13) we were given as the readers of Mark a supernatural insight into the true identity of Jesus. At the beginning of this second part we are given in two verses a summary of the whole mission of Jesus.

After John is handed over, which already prefigures Jesus' own end, Jesus came announcing the good news of God. It is 'of' God because it is 'from' God and because it is 'about' God. The gospel, a word from the old English, 'god-spel' meaning good news, is immediately not something we are commanded to do. Nor is it simply a message. The gospel is the power of God, something God does.

The divine action of God becomes visible in the human words, human actions and, above all, in the human personality of Jesus. Jesus made the gospel of God uniquely audible, visible and tangible by his words, his actions, and by the kind of person he habitually was. Actions proclaim the gospel louder than words, but persons proclaim the good news of God's action loudest of all.

The gospel is God giving us life, God healing our human brokenness, and God bringing the differences and diversity of the world into unity and harmony. It is the good news that God continues to be our creator, our redeemer or liberator, and our reconciler.

The favourite phrase of Jesus for the gospel was the 'kingdom of God'. The kingdom already begins to become a visible place in the world when it is genuinely proclaimed, as Jesus proclaimed it, by words, by actions, or by a personal witness of life.

The kingdom of God also begins to be visible in the world wherever people respond to God's initiating action by a radical turning, or conversion, from self to God, and continue to respond by their believing, or 'faithing', in the gospel.

Mark 1:16-20

16 As Jesus passed along the Sea of Galilee, he saw Simon and his brother Andrew casting a net into the sea — for they were fishermen.

17 And Jesus said to them, 'Follow me and I will make you fish for people.'

18 And immediately they left their nets and followed him.

19 As he went a little further, he saw James the son of Zebedee and his brother John, who were in their boat mending the nets.

20 Immediately he called them; and they left their father Zebedee in the boat with the hired men, and followed him.

Starters

1. *Why do I think Mark has put this story at the beginning of the mission of Jesus to bring the good news of God to the world?*

2. *Let me imagine myself in the place of Simon or Andrew. What do I feel when Jesus unexpectedly calls me to be with him and share his mission?*

3. *Try to feel how attractive for the disciples must have been the person of Jesus, and their enthusiasm as they left their boats to follow him.*

II/2. Jesus calls the first disciples

After the identity of Jesus himself, the response of the disciples is the second key factor in Mark's Gospel. Two questions continually challenge us. Who is Jesus? What is the response to him?

The decisive element in this passage is the call of Jesus, not the response of the two pairs of brothers. Nothing is said about the qualities of the men he calls or their suitability to be companions with him in his mission.

Jewish disciples sought out a master to study under him for a time, but Jesus himself seeks out followers. He does not call them to study but to be with him always. By following him they observe his work, listen to his teaching and begin to be challenged by him.

Simon and Andrew are casting into the lake, probably with a circular net. Mark always names him Simon in this first chapter of his Gospel. Jesus calls them to be a different kind of fishermen. They are to leave their nets and follow him. Obviously Mark has simplified and dramatised the actual historical event, but two things are clear. The disciples are called to be with Jesus and to share his mission.

A little further along the lakeshore, James and John are mending their fishing-nets. They too are called and respond at once. A change in relations with their families and in their customary way of working is singled out in the few details Mark mentions. To follow Jesus as disciples means leaving many familiar things behind. The unexpected call of the four fishermen is like the call of Elisha by Elijah (1 Kings 19:19-21).

Following Jesus in Mark means more than physical companionship. It is feeling the costly challenges of the new liberating power Jesus brings to the world. Nor will it always be easy attraction and instant response. There are shocks in store for the disciples.

21 They went to Capernaum; and when the sabbath came, he entered the synagogue and taught. 22 They were astounded at his teaching, for he taught them as one having authority, and not as the scribes.

23 Just then there was in their synagogue a man with an unclean spirit, 24 and he cried out, 'What have you to do with us, Jesus of Nazareth? Have you come to destroy us? I know who you are, the Holy One of God.' 25 But Jesus rebuked him, saying, 'Be silent, and come out of him!' 26 And the unclean spirit, convulsing him and crying with a loud voice, came out of him. 27 They were all amazed, and they kept on asking one another, 'What is this? A new teaching — with authority! He commands even the unclean spirits, and they obey him.' 28 At once his fame began to spread throughout the surrounding region of Galilee.

29 As soon as they left the synagogue, they entered the house of Simon and Andrew, with James and John. 30 Now Simon's mother-in-law was in bed with a fever, and they told him about her at once. 31 He came and took her by the hand and lifted her up. Then the fever left her; and she began to serve them.

32 That evening, at sundown, they brought to him all who were sick or possessed with demons. 33 And the whole city was gathered together around the door. 34 And he cured many who were sick with various diseases, and cast out many demons; and he would not permit the demons to speak, because they knew him.

35 In the morning, while it was still very dark, he got up and went out to a deserted place, and there he prayed. 36 And Simon and his companions hunted for him. 37 When they found him, they said to him, 'Everyone is searching for you.' 38 He answered, 'Let us go on to the neighbouring towns, so that I may proclaim the message there also; for that is what I came out to do.' 39 And he went throughout all Galilee, proclaiming the message in their synagogues and casting out demons.

II/3. A day in the life of Jesus

The first disciples have been called and they are with Jesus, watching him, as we are.

What we see first is Jesus attacking evils that hold people captive, dehumanising and alienating them from society. Within the broad outlines of a day in the life of Jesus Mark presents four connected episodes. They bear traces of the vivid imagery of early cherished memories from eye-witnesses.

The day begins with Jesus teaching in the synagogue, and all are amazed for he teaches not like the scribes who repeat what they have learnt from books, but with authority, as one with real power. When a madman shrieks out that Jesus from Nazareth is the Holy One of God, or Messiah, Jesus dramatically cures him, but silences the demon. Mark's Gospel implies that a demon knows in some way Jesus is the Messiah.

From the synagogue Jesus goes to Simon's house where he at once completely cures the mother of Simon's wife with the same power.

After sunset, at the end of the Sabbath, the sick of Capernaum are brought to this house of Simon, and Jesus cures many different kinds of illness and mental trouble. Mark, by showing Jesus silencing the demons, implies that the true nature of the Messiah can be known only through faith given by God.

Next morning, we find Jesus praying in a lonely place. His prayer points to the source of his power and authority. Perhaps also it is through this kind of prayerful union with God that Jesus in his humanness draws strength to leave Capernaum, where he is welcomed and sought, and take the gospel to other places where he may not be welcomed. So begins for Jesus many days of bringing the gospel in the synagogues of Galilee and of freeing people from the evils in their lives.

Mark 1:40-45

40 *A leper came to him begging him, and kneeling he said to him, 'If you choose, you can make me clean.'*

41 *Moved with pity, Jesus stretched out his hand and touched him, and said to him, 'I do choose. Be made clean!'*

42 *Immediately the leprosy left him, and he was made clean.*

43 *After sternly warning him he sent him away at once,* **44** *saying to him, 'See that you say nothing to anyone; but go, show yourself to the priest, and offer for your cleansing what Moses commanded, as a testimony to them.'*

45 *But he went out and began to proclaim it freely, and to spread the word, so that Jesus could no longer go into a town openly, but stayed out in the country; and people came to him from every quarter.*

Starters

1. *Try to share the interior feeling of Jesus when he was moved to pity, or, as some of the early versions have, moved to anger?*

2. *Consider a little who might be the lepers, the outcasts or marginalised, in society today and in what way Jesus can come to them in our times.*

II/4. Jesus heals a leper

The story of the healing of a leper is another episode of Jesus attacking evil in the world with authority and divine power. Possibly Mark has placed it here to link two sections which he may have found as collections of stories already existing in an early community tradition. The first section contains stories of a day in the life of Jesus at Capernaum, upon which we have just reflected (1:21-39), the second is a series of stories about conflicts of Jesus with scribes, which we are yet to read (2:1 — 3:6).

In the time of Jesus, leprosy covered a variety of skin diseases. For the Jews, leprosy had always been an uncleanness which prevented persons from sharing in ritual worship and in normal social life. Their concern was the protection of the rest of the community rather than the unfortunate sufferers themselves, as the Old Testament makes clear (Lev 13-14). Jesus has a different view.

Jesus shows himself to be one who comes to outcast and marginal people. He is also one who shows respect and obedience for social laws and community traditions instituted for the welfare of all.

We read that Jesus felt a movement of deep compassion within himself when he heard the cries of the leper and saw him kneeling before him. There are indications in the early manuscripts of Mark's Gospel that Mark may have originally written that Jesus 'felt anger' when he saw the leper, and that this was later altered to 'felt compassion'. An anger in Jesus against evil fits better the spirit of Mark's Gospel where Jesus personifies in himself God breaking into our world to free it from evil and human injustices.

The cure of the leper by Jesus is a witness by Jesus to God's concern for the total good of every person and a full participation for everyone in social life and community living.

Mark 2:1-12

1 When he returned to Capernaum after some days, it was reported that he was at home. 2 So many gathered around that there was no longer room for them, not even in front of the door; and he was speaking the word to them.

3 Then some people came, bringing to him a paralysed man, carried by four of them. 4 And when they could not bring him to Jesus because of the crowd, they removed the roof above him; and after having dug through it, they let down the mat on which the paralytic lay.

5 When Jesus saw their faith, he said to the paralytic, 'Son, your sins are forgiven.'

6 Now some of the scribes were sitting there, questioning in their hearts, 7 'Why does this fellow speak in this way? It is blasphemy! Who can forgive sins but God alone?'

8 At once Jesus perceived in his spirit that they were discussing these questions among themselves; and he said to them, 'Why do you raise such questions in your hearts? 9 Which is easier, to say to the paralytic, "Your sins are forgiven," or to say, "Stand up and take up your mat and walk"? 10 But so that you may know that the Son of Man has authority on earth to forgive sins' — he said to the paralytic — 11 'I say to you, stand up, take your mat and go to your home.'

12 And he stood up, and immediately took the mat and went out before all of them; so that they were all amazed and glorified God, saying, 'We have never seen anything like this!'

Starters

1. *Let me imagine the person on the stretcher is myself. Who might be the four persons I would ask to carry me to Jesus?*
2. *Exodus 34:6-7, Isaiah 43:25, or Psalm 51:1-2 might help you to pray this passage more personally.*

II/5. Jesus heals a paralytic

With Chapter Two we begin a series of five conflicts (2:1 — 3:6). Mark is at pains to show how opposition to Jesus began early and grew steadily. These stories emphasise the surprising newness and unique authority of the teaching of Jesus. They also show the widening gap between Jesus and the scribes and pharisees, the recognised teachers and authorities in the Jewish religion of his day.

Jesus has returned to Capernaum, on the northern shore of Lake Galilee, where apparently he has made his home in the house of Simon (1:29). People crowd to hear him. Four friends bring a paralysed man on a simple bed, but they cannot reach Jesus. The friends are determined and adventurous. They dig a hole in the mud roof and let down the stretcher, right in front of Jesus.

When he sees their faith, Jesus shocks everyone, especially the teachers of the law, when he speaks with affection and forgives the man's sins! For the Jews, only God forgives sins. The outraged questioning of the scribes is highlighted, or 'framed', according to the Hebrew literary fashion, by the forgiveness of the man's sins before and the cure of his paralysis after.

The Christians of Mark's time believed, as we do, that Christ as the risen Lord continues to forgive sins in and through the present actions of the church. The Jews understood forgiveness of sins more as a future good from God for which to hope. Jesus shows this future good has already come into the world in himself.

Jesus makes the cure of the man's paralysis the sign of a more radical freeing from dehumanising evil and bondage, his sinfulness. He acts with God's own power. The man, walking away with the stretcher under his arm, dramatically contrasts with the start of the story when the same man lay helpless on the stretcher carried by the four others.

Mark 2:13-17

13 Jesus went out again beside the sea; and the whole crowd gathered around him, and he taught them.

14 As he was walking along, he saw Levi son of Alphaeus sitting at the tax booth, and he said to him, 'Follow me.' And he got up and followed him.

15 And as he sat at dinner in Levi's house, many tax collectors and sinners were also sitting with Jesus and his disciples — for there were many who followed him.

16 When the scribes of the Pharisees saw that he was eating with sinners and tax collectors, they said to his disciples, 'Why does he eat with tax collectors and sinners?'

17 When Jesus heard this, he said to them, 'Those who are well have no need of a physician, but those who are sick; I have come to call not the righteous, but sinners.'

Starters

1. *Why do you think Jesus does not identify himself with the scribes and Pharisees, the acknowledged scholars and spiritual leaders?*

2. *God in the Old Testament is a healer and liberator from evil. Consider some examples: Hosea 14:5, Isaiah 61:1, Jeremiah 30:17.*

II/6. Jesus eats with the irreligious

This second conflict story has two parts. First, there is the story of Levi, reduced to its bare outline, probably by re-telling among early Christians over a number of years. In its unexpectedness it is similar to the earlier call of the first four disciples (1:16-20).

When Mark later lists the Twelve, he does not include Levi (3:16-19), so perhaps when he wrote his Gospel in the '60s there was some confusion in the tradition about Jesus on the position of Levi as a disciple. The Gospel of Matthew seems to identify Levi with Matthew himself (Mt 9:9).

In the second part of the story, Jesus shares a meal with taxcollectors, probably friends of Levi, who were considered social outcasts by most Jews, and with sinners, probably ordinary people who did not observe the law with the same strictness as the scribes did. Mark seems to say that the meal takes place in the house of Jesus himself at Capernaum. He also says there are already many disciples of Jesus — not many tax-collectors and sinners.

This is the second time we see Jesus sharing a meal with his disciples (1:31). 'Disciple' is an important and frequently used word in Mark's Gospel. The Old Testament prophets like Elijah did not have disciples, but servants (1 Kings 19:21). Notable rabbis at the time of Jesus had disciples, but the disciples of Jesus are especially characterised by their being with him always and sharing with him all he does.

Many scribes were also Pharisees who are mentioned here by Mark for the first time. They see Jesus eating with tax-collectors and other people not particularly religious. Again they are shocked and question his disciples. To accept Jesus as the one who heals with new life and forgives with God's forgiveness ordinary, struggling people is too much for these religious authorities to accept.

18 Now John's disciples and the Pharisees were fasting; and people came and said to him, 'Why do John's disciples and the disciples of the Pharisees fast, but your disciples do not fast?'

19 Jesus said to them, 'The wedding guests cannot fast while the bridegroom is with them, can they? As long as they have the bridegroom with them, they cannot fast.

20 'The days will come, when the bridegroom is taken away from them, and then they will fast on that day.

21 'No one sews a piece of unshrunk cloth on an old cloak; otherwise, the patch pulls away from it, the new from the old, and a worse tear is made.

22 'And no one puts new wine into old wineskins; otherwise, the wine will burst the skins, and the wine is lost, and so are the skins; but one puts new wine into fresh wineskins.'

Starters

1. Verify that this episode is the centrepiece of the five conflict stories and so contains their central teaching.

2. Reflect on places in the Bible where God is the bridegroom of Israel: Hosea 2:19-20, Isaiah 62:5, Jeremiah 2:2, Ezekiel 16:8.

3. Consider ways that I may be trying to fit the new thing God is doing into narrow understandings of life or limited ways of living?

II /7. Jesus is asked about fasting

The third conflict, which may at first look commonplace, is the centrepiece of the five. In the Hebrew way of organising a literary work, which Mark follows, the central passage is the focus where the most important teaching is placed.

Two stories of new teachings of Jesus are positioned on either side and 'frame' this central story. Also two emphatic references to Jesus as the mysterious Son of man are equally placed on either side of this central episode (2:10 and 28).

The story begins when some people, neither scribes nor Pharisees, so it seems, question Jesus about why he and his disciples are not fasting. Jesus replies that he is like a bridegroom among his disciples who will not be with them always in the way he is now. Opposition to Jesus will lead eventually to his separation from the disciples by death. Only then will the real newness of what he brings be revealed clearly to his disciples.

The Old Testament never describes the Messiah as a bridegroom. For the prophets, the bridegroom of Israel is always God himself. This is why what Jesus brings cannot be compared with what John or the Pharisees, or the Jewish religion, can offer. Jesus by his teaching and his actions, and in his very person, brings to the world in a new and unique way the personal presence and action of God, the Spouse of Israel. No wonder the people find the teaching of Jesus so new and his authority so different from that of the scribes (2:22 and 27).

This central teaching of Jesus is reinforced by two short parables, or comparisons, which end the episode. Patching clothes with new, unshrunken cloth, or trying to put new wine into old, hardened wineskins is a waste. The new power Jesus brings into the world cannot be quietly fitted into what the old religion gives.

23 *One sabbath he was going through the grainfields; and as they made their way his disciples began to pluck heads of grain.*

24 *The Pharisees said to him, 'Look, why are they doing what is not lawful on the sabbath?'*

25 *And he said to them, 'Have you never read what David did when he and his companions were hungry and in need of food?*

26 *'He entered the house of God, when Abiathar was high priest, and ate the bread of the Presence, which it is not lawful for any but the priests to eat, and he gave some to his companions.'*

27 *Then he said to them, 'The sabbath was made for human-kind, and not humankind for the sabbath; 28 so the Son of Man is Lord even of the sabbath.'*

Starters

1. *Ponder what Jesus teaches here: at the heart of the life of a true disciple is not a law but a personal relation with himself.*

2. *See how often Jesus calls himself 'Son of Man': 2:10, 28, 8:31, 38, 9:9, 12, 31, 10:33, 45, 13:26, 14:21 (twice), 41, 62.*

II/8. Jesus defends a human need

The first two of the five conflicts concerned sinners. The last two concern the Jewish Sabbath. The same balance is found in the opponents of Jesus, who in the first two stories are the scribes but in the last two are the Pharisees.

The fourth conflict is not in a town but in the cornfields near the Lake of Galilee. When the disciples begin to pick corn as they walk along, the Pharisees point out to Jesus that this is forbidden on the Sabbath.

Jesus attacks them by showing how laws have their limits, even the sacred law of the Sabbath rest. He recalls to the Pharisees what David once did in the time of the priest Abiathar, actually Ahimelech, when he and his men were hungry (1 Sam 21:1-6).

Jesus shocks the Pharisees by authoritatively interpreting the letter of God's Law in favour of the hunger of his disciples. Even the sacred law of the Sabbath he puts aside for the sake of their human need. The concern of Jesus reveals God's central concern with life and the welfare of persons.

Notice how Jesus refers to himself by the puzzling title Son of Man. This title for Jesus is often found in Mark's Gospel, mostly in the second half, and only on the lips of Jesus himself.

Son of Man, or 'Bar Nasha' in the Aramaic language which Jesus spoke, seems to be the special word of Jesus for himself as human like the rest of us but in a way that makes people wonder and question further.

At the end of the first of the five 'Conflict Stories' Jesus presented himself as the Son of Man with authority to forgive sins (2:10). Now, just before the beginning of the fifth and final story, Jesus presents himself again as the Son of Man with authority over the Sabbath (2:28).

Mark 3:1-6

1 Again he entered the synagogue, and a man was there who had a withered hand.

2 They watched him to see whether he would cure him on the sabbath, so that they might accuse him.

3 And he said to the man who had the withered hand, 'Come forward'.

4 Then he said to them, 'Is it lawful to do good or to do harm on the sabbath, to save life or to kill?' But they were silent.

5 He looked around at them with anger; he was grieved at their hardness of heart and said to the man, 'Stretch out your hand.' He stretched it out, and his hand was restored.

6 The Pharisees went out, and immediately conspired with the Herodians against him, how to destroy him.

Starters

1. Contrast the positive towards life of Jesus with the narrow attitudes of religious and political leaders opposing him.

2. Try to feel something of what Jesus felt when he saw the attitudes of the Pharisees and the Herodians.

II/9. Jesus heals a paralysed hand

The last of the five conflicts, like the first, is caused by a healing done by Jesus. Again he deliberately confronts his opponents. These are presumably the Pharisees mentioned at the end of the story. They look, waiting to see if Jesus will heal the man with a paralysed and shrunken hand.

Ignoring the opposition, Jesus tells the deformed man to come and stand in front of everyone. The Jews did interpret the Sabbath law to allow action to heal the sick but only when there was danger to life. Jesus is more radical, 'Is it allowed on the Sabbath to do good or do harm?' As he puts to them this simple question, he looks around upon his silent opponents with a strong feeling of anger, because he sees hardness of heart and a refusal to understand. Mark has mentioned the emotions of Jesus once before (1:41).

Dramatically, in full view of the Pharisees, Jesus heals the man's paralysed limb. Again he acts with power and authority.

This story may also reflect a more liberal attitude of early Jewish Christians in Mark's day towards the Sabbath as a practice that was based on the behaviour and a clear teaching of Jesus. For Christians Sunday became the special day of the week.

The final result of this new teaching of Jesus and the dramatic healing he performed is not wonder among the people but rejection by his opponents. The Pharisees, religious leaders, join together with the Herodians, political leaders, and go off to plot his death. Such radically new teachings of Jesus endanger both the traditional teachings of the Jewish religion as well as the established structures of Jewish politics under Roman domination. This malice and ill-will towards Jesus will be there throughout the rest of his time in Galilee, and reach its terrible climax later in Jerusalem.

III

JESUS WITH THE PEOPLE

Mark 3:7 — 6:6a

7 Jesus departed with his disciples to the sea, and a great multitude from Galilee followed him; hearing all that he was doing, they came to him in great numbers from Judea, Jerusalem, Idumea, beyond the Jordan, and the region around Tyre and Sidon.

9 He told his disciples to have a boat ready for him because of the crowd, so that they would not crush him; 10 for he had cured many, so that all who had diseases pressed upon him to touch him.

11 Whenever the unclean spirits saw him, they fell down before him and shouted, 'You are the Son of God!'

12 But he sternly ordered them not to make him known.

Starters

1. *The demons named Jesus Son of God. Reflect a while to see what I really mean when I name Jesus 'Son of God'.*

2. *Try to feel and resonate with something of the enthusiasm and confusion of the people around Jesus as he taught at the lakeside.*

3. *Compare again the other occasions when Jesus is named Son of God, twice by God (1:11, 9:7), and in four other places (1:1, 5:7, 14:61, 15:39).*

III/1. Summary: the crowds around Jesus

As in the second part, a summary passage begins a third part of Mark's Gospel. This third part describes the work and mission of Jesus as its height. Jesus withdraws again (1:45), this time to the shore of Lake Galilee. Hearing from others about all he was doing, the crowds flock to him there from all over Galilee, and from Jerusalem and other distant regions.

'Hearing' the word, or the gospel, brought by Jesus is a key theme recurring throughout this third part of Mark's Gospel. Till now the crowds have heard his word from others, not from Jesus himself.

In this opening summary passage, the people crowd around Jesus with wild enthusiasm, pressing tightly against him. Those troubled with diseases try to touch him, for he has freed people from many different kinds of evil. They sense a new power in him. So many have come that there is danger he will be crushed by the crowds. He asks his disciples to have a boat ready on the lake. He may need to move from the shore.

Mad people fall on the ground in front of him, shrieking that he is the Son of God! Mark states again his strange view that the demons know the truth which Christians believe about Jesus, and which the reader already knows from the Gospel prologue (1:13), but which the crowds and the disciples have not yet discovered.

Mark emphasises again that Jesus silences the demons and will not let them make known his true identity. The people and his disciples have not yet experienced Jesus deeply enough, it seems, to believe what the title 'Son of God' really means.

Jesus is truly known as the Son of God only by believers. Through their faith they can recognise in his person and liberating service of others God's own life and action coming into the world.

13 He went up the mountain, and called to him those whom he wanted; and they came to him.

14 And he appointed twelve, whom he also named apostles, to be with him, and to be sent out to proclaim the message, 15 and to have authority to cast out demons.

16 So he appointed the twelve: Simon (to whom he gave the name Peter);

17 James son of Zebedee and John the brother of James (to whom he gave the name Boanerges), that is, Sons of Thunder;

18 and Andrew, and Philip, and Bartholomew, and Matthew, and Thomas, and James son of Alphaeus, and Thaddaeus, and Simon the Cananaean,

19 and Judas Iscariot, who betrayed him.

Starters

1. *Look at Jesus alone on the mountain and try to feel something of his own interior experience of God and the way he might speak with God.*

2. *What would it mean for you to be with Jesus and yet sent by him?*

III/2. Jesus appoints the twelve

After the summary opening of the second part, Jesus called four disciples. Again after a summary opening to this third part he appoints from his disciples the twelve.

A mountain, from the time of Moses on Mount Sinai, is a place to meet God. There Jesus calls his disciples to him, to come and share his experience of God. To come away to him, they must leave something behind. Jesus makes twelve, a symbol of the twelve tribes of Israel, to be a new chosen people to work with him for the kingdom of God coming into the world. He gives new names to the first three to signify a new identity.

The mission of the twelve is to preach, implicitly the gospel, although Mark does not directly say this. In Mark's Gospel, during his historical life only Jesus explicitly proclaims the gospel of the kingdom of God. The disciples and John the baptiser preach a radical conversion of heart, or *'metanoia'*.

The preaching is confirmed by a second task of their mission, to drive out demons, or to free persons from all that dehumanises them. This can include any kind of unwanted poverty: material poverty through lack of food, clothing or shelter; social poverty when persons suffer discrimination or lack a voice in society; physical poverty from bodily illness, deformities or old age; mental poverty through a lack of education, crippling anxieties or mental illnesses; and spiritual poverty through a lack of God's Spirit enabling persons to receive and give love.

The twelve chosen by Jesus are individually named. Though all are men, almost certainly for cultural reasons, this naming reminds all of us, men or women, of the deep biblical sense of naming. To be named by Jesus is to be personally involved with him then as the human Jesus, now in our time as the risen Lord.

20 *Then he went home; and the crowd came together again, so that they could not even eat.* 21 *When his family heard it, they went out to restrain him, for people were saying, 'He has gone out of his mind.'*

22 *And the scribes who came down from Jerusalem said, 'He has Beelzebul, and by the ruler of the demons he casts out demons.'* 23 *And he called them to him, and spoke to them in parables, 'How can Satan cast out Satan?* 24 *If a kingdom is divided against itself, that kingdom cannot stand.* 25 *And if a house is divided against itself, that house will not be able to stand.* 26 *And if Satan has risen up against himself and is divided, he cannot stand, but his end has come.* 27 *But no one can enter a strong man's house and plunder his property without first tying up the strong man; then indeed the house can be plundered.*

28 *'Truly, I tell you, people will be forgiven for their sins and whatever blasphemies they utter;* 29 *but whoever blasphemes against the Holy Spirit can never have forgiveness, but is guilty of an eternal sin'* — 30 *for they had said, 'He has an unclean spirit.'*

31 *Then his mother and his brothers came; and standing outside they sent to him and called him.* 32 *A crowd was sitting around him; and they said to him, 'Your mother and your brothers and sisters are outside, asking for you.'* 33 *And he replied, 'Who are my mother and my brothers?'* 34 *And looking at those who sat around him, he said, 'Here are my mother and my brothers!* 35 *Whoever does the will of God is my brother and sister and mother.'*

Starters

1. *Ponder here the strangeness that the family saw in Jesus now that he has begun to act in this new way.*

2. *How really in my heart do I feel that I would still be free if God's will truly became my will?*

III/3. Opposition to Jesus grows

Jesus returns home, to the lakeside town of Capernaum. The opposition to him continues to grow from two sources, the fears of his family for his sanity, and the malice of the scribes from Jerusalem.

Mark uses one of his favourite literary devices. He 'sandwiches' one story within another, the opposition of the scribes (3:22-30) within the opposition of the family of Jesus.

The scribes from Jerusalem say Jesus uses the power of Beelzebul, a name for Satan as the prince of demons. Jesus speaks to them in parables, or comparisons, of which Mark gives only brief summaries. Can Satan fight Satan? A kingdom divided cannot last. A divided house falls. A strong man's home can be burgled only if someone first binds the strong man. Jesus, we saw, comes as the one to bind Satan and free people from his evil power.

Jesus sees the scribes opposing him as resisting the Holy Spirit. To resist the Holy Spirit of God is to resist the only power by which a person can begin to experience life as it really is.

The so-called 'sin against the Holy Spirit' is unforgivable, not because God is unwilling to forgive, but because persons refuse to recognise the presence of God's power breaking into the world, and to welcome its liberating action into their own lives.

When the family of Jesus arrives, they stand as outsiders, with the opposition not with the disciples. This is the first time we see the mother and brothers of Jesus in Mark's Gospel, but Mark gives us no further information about them. His concern is elsewhere.

'Who are my real family?' Jesus asks. Mark wants to emphasise that the real family of Jesus are the ones who are with him as disciples, the ones sitting around listening to him, those to whom he can reveal the secret of the kingdom of God.

Mark 4:1-12

1 Again he began to teach beside the sea. Such a very large crowd gathered around him, that he got into a boat on the sea and sat there, while the whole crowd was beside the sea on the land.

2 He began to teach them many things in parables, and in his teaching he said to them:

3 'Listen! A sower went out to sow. 4 And as he sowed, some seed fell on the path, and the birds came and ate it up. 5 Other seed fell on rocky ground, where it did not have much soil, and it sprang up quickly, since it had no depth of soil. 6 And when the sun rose, it was scorched; and since it had no root, it withered away. 7 Other seed fell among thorns, and the thorns grew up and choked it, and it yielded no grain. 8 Other seed fell into good soil and brought forth grain, growing up and increasing and yielding thirty and sixty and a hundredfold.'

9 And he said, 'Let anyone with ears to hear listen!'

10 When he was alone, those who were around him along with the twelve asked him about the parables.

11 And he said to them, 'To you has been given the secret of the kingdom of God, but for those outside, everything comes in parables; 12 in order that they may indeed look but not perceive, and may indeed listen but not understand; so that they may not turn again, and be forgiven.'

Starters

1. *Search for some of the ways in which this power of God, which Jesus calls the kingdom of God, may be entering my life at the present time.*

2. *What do these impossibly rich harvests in the good soil teach me about the kingdom of God coming into the world?*

III/4. The parable of a sower

So many people crowd around Jesus at the lakeside that he gets into a boat which earlier he asked his disciples to have ready (3:9). From the boat he teaches the people standing along the shore in parables.

Parables were used by Jesus, as they were by the rabbis and other teachers of his time, as ways of coming to know a mystery through a comparison with some familiar situation already known.

The comparison could be made through a story or simply by a brief metaphor or allusion. When the comparison was made in a short, catchy way, it was a proverb. A parable became a riddle or puzzle, when people failed to experience the insight or the mystery it introduced. The parable-comparisons of Jesus become parable-puzzles to those without faith in the mysterious action of God in the world.

This parable of the sower compares the coming of God into the world with the situation of a sower scattering seed for a harvest. It seems that the farmers of Israel at the time of Jesus sowed the seed before, not after, they ploughed the land. Though God's power may appear to be wasted or destroyed, it eventually produces wonderful results. The parable begins and ends with a call to listen (4:3 and 9).

Strangely, Mark seems to say that Jesus told parables as a deliberately puzzling way of teaching to hide from the outsiders the true meaning of the kingdom (4:10-12).

This is part of Mark's emphasis on a reluctance of Jesus to accept in public the title of Messiah, and an unwillingness in him to reveal to all his true identity. In fact, Jesus told parables to lead people by faith to a personal discovery in their own lives of the kingdom of God revealed in his own person, and to stir a radical commitment in all to its coming into the world.

53

13 And he said to them, 'Do you not understand this parable? Then how will you understand all the parables?

14 'The sower sows the word.

15 'These are the ones on the path, where the word is sown: when they hear, Satan immediately comes and takes away the word that is sown in them.

16 'And these are the ones sown on rocky ground: when they hear the word, they immediately receive it with joy. 17 But they have no root, and endure only for a while; then, when trouble or persecution arises on account of the word, immediately they fall away.

18 'And others are those sown among the thorns: these are the ones who hear the word, 19 but the cares of the world, and the lure of wealth, and the desire for other things come in and choke the word, and it yields nothing.

20 'And these are the ones sown on the good soil: they hear the word and accept it and bear fruit, thirty and sixty and a hundredfold.'

Starters

1. *Ponder the four different dispositions towards the gospel of God which are symbolised by the four kinds of soil where the seed fell.*

2. *In which of the four classes of hearers would I place myself at this present time of my life?*

III/5. An allegory of the sower

This explanation of the parable of the sower sowing seed is an example of what people generally call an allegory. A parable is a story which simply compares a known situation with a less known or unknown situation. An allegory does more. It is a further development of a parable where each detail is given a meaning.

Preachers and story-tellers today often allegorise traditional stories to deepen and enrich our understanding of them and to help us apply in a practical manner the truth they contain. It is probable that Mark found in the community where he lived this allegorical development of the parable of Jesus about the sower.

Jesus may, of course, have also made an allegory of the sower. More likely, Mark has put upon the lips of Jesus a traditional explanation of the parable Jesus actually told, which was already current in the early Christian communities and which was judged to be faithful to the meaning of the original story of Jesus (4:1-9).

In the allegory the focus is changed from the coming of the kingdom of God to the different ways in which people 'hear' or respond to the kingdom. Notice how often the word 'hearing' occurs.

Hearing the meaning of a parable is for those who listen with true faith. The hardened soil of a well-trodden path is the stubbornness of heart which Satan puts in some people and which prevents any hearing at all of God's Word. The rocky ground is shallowness of character in some hearers. The thorns are the cares of the world which drastically diminish a person's capacity to listen in freedom to the deeper realities of life.

The thirty, sixty and hundredfold harvest are people who really hear the Gospel and respond by bearing fruit in their lives in differing degrees, but always with extraordinary results, quite beyond any human expectation.

21 He said to them, 'Is a lamp brought in to be put under the bushel basket, or under the bed, and not on the lampstand?

22 'For there is nothing hidden, except to be disclosed; nor is anything secret, except to come to light.

23 'Let anyone who has ears to hear listen!'

24 And he said to them, 'Pay attention to what you hear; the measure you give will be the measure you get, and still more will be given you.

25 'For to those who have, more will be given; and from those who have nothing, even what they have will be taken away.'

Starters

1. Reflect how these two parables of the lamp and the measuring basket teach something about how God's power comes into people.

2. Consider how the power which the gospel of God brings into the world depends to a large degree on how men and women welcome it.

III/6. Parables of a lamp and a measure

In this passage, which contains the two parable-proverbs of the lamp and the measure, Mark has probably placed together five sayings of Jesus, which may have been spoken by him in different situations.

Four of the sayings are grouped in pairs, which Mark may have found already grouped that way in the community tradition which was given to him. The fifth saying, which Mark also uses elsewhere (4:9), by its central position (4:23) becomes the focus and the key for the reader to understand the whole passage.

The kingdom of God, the divine action coming into our human world, is not meant to remain hidden. Nobody lights a lamp to hide it under a basket for measuring grain or under a bed, but puts it on a stand where it can shed its light around.

The kingdom of God may at first seem hidden in the words and actions and humble life of Jesus, but it will soon spread far and wide in his disciples as a light shining throughout the world.

Like the parable of the lamp, the parable of the measuring basket also points to the way persons welcome and respond to the kingdom of God coming into their lives. The degree to which one gives to others and is open to the need of others is a direct measure and indicator of the degree to which God can share with that person his divine action. A person closed to another by that very fact shows a heart closed against God. One's giving to others measures one's receiving from God.

The more people welcome God's action into their lives, the more they are able to receive God's further action. There is no injustice here. It is simply a question of one's capacity and willingness to receive. The limit is on our side, not on God's!

Mark 4:26-34

26 He also said, 'The kingdom of God is as if someone would scatter seed on the ground, 27 and would sleep and rise night and day, and the seed would sprout and grow, he does not know how.

28 'The earth produces of itself, first the stalk, then the head, then the full grain in the head.

29 'But when the grain is ripe, at once he goes in with his sickle, because the harvest has come.'

30 He also said, 'With what can we compare the kingdom of God, or what parable will we use for it?

31 'It is like a mustard seed, which, when sown upon the ground, is the smallest of all the seeds on earth; 32 yet when it is sown it grows up and becomes the greatest of all shrubs, and puts forth large branches, so that the birds of the air can make nests in its shade.'

33 With many such parables he spoke the word to them, as they were able to hear it; 34 he did not speak to them except in parables, but he explained everything in private to his disciples.

Starters

1. Take a little time to look at some natural growing thing and compare it with God's power coming into the world.

2. Look into your own life at the present time and see if you can recognise any hidden or small beginnings of the kingdom.

III/7. A growing seed and a mustard plant

These two parables, like the three previous ones, are taken from agricultural situations known to his Galilean listeners.

The parable of the growing seeds is found only in Mark's Gospel. The farmer throws the seeds carelessly into the ground and goes off to do other things, but seeds have an inner vitality. They sprout and grow, first the stalk, then the head coming from the stalk, and finally the ripe grain of wheat within the head.

The tiny mustard seed, smaller than other seeds, grows surely and steadily into a shrub, three to four metres high with large branches, in the shade of which birds can come and sit. What a large result from such a tiny beginning!

Both parables reveal the kingdom of God as a growth from small and insignificant beginnings. The scattered seeds grow with an inner vitality of their own until the harvest. The tiny mustard seed grows to produce a large shrub, out of all proportion to the tiny seed that was sown. These parables give insights into the way the kingdom of God grows in the world — the small beginnings, the steady, silent growth, until finally the abundant and surprising results. The action of God in Jesus may seem small and hardly noticeable, yet its great fruits will inevitably appear.

In our devotion we might also prayerfully ponder how Jesus could look around him at the small group of disciples and the people who hung upon his words and feel a hope for the future.

Mark concludes by reminding us that this collection of five parables is only a small sample of the parables which Jesus told. The parables offer understanding and faith to the degree each can grasp and interiorise what is heard. Parables puzzle unbelievers, but give disciples deeper insights into the kingdom of God.

35 On that day, when evening had come, he said to them, 'Let us go across to the other side.'

36 And leaving the crowd behind, they took him with them in the boat, just as he was. Other boats were with him.

37 A great windstorm arose, and the waves beat into the boat, so that the boat was already being swamped.

38 But he was in the stern, asleep on the cushion; and they woke him up and said to him, 'Teacher, do you not care that we are perishing?'

39 He woke up and rebuked the wind, and said to the sea, 'Peace! Be still!' Then the wind ceased, and there was a dead calm.

40 He said to them, 'Why are you afraid? Have you still no faith?'

41 And they were filled with great awe, and said to one another, 'Who then is this, that even the wind and the sea obey him?'

Starters

1. Imagine the scene of the storm-tossed boat in the waves and notice what you begin to see and feel in yourself.

2. Try to share something of the shock and terror of the disciples when they saw what power Jesus used over the wind.

III/8. Jesus calms the storm

After a sample of five parables to show how Jesus taught the people about the kingdom of God (4:1-34), Mark gives five examples of how Jesus made the kingdom visible by actions that shocked people and made them wonder (4:35—6:6).

Jesus asks his disciples to take him over to the eastern shore of the lake. Since he is already in the boat, they take him just as he is. Suddenly, there is a great storm of wind. They wake Jesus and say they are sinking. With great power he commands the wind and the sea and there is calm.

If this story is compared with the way it is told in Matthew (Mt 8:23-27), it becomes clear how the focus in Mark's version is on the divine power acting through Jesus and the terror of this power in the disciples.

The power of the kingdom breaks into their lives. In Matthew there is fear in the disciples before Jesus acts, but what they feel afterwards is wonder, not the great fear described in Mark. Mark's has told the story almost like a cosmic exorcism of the evil in the storm.

Control over the wind and the sea in the Old Testament belongs to God as the Creator of the world (Genesis) and the Redeemer of Israel (Exodus). The action of Jesus is not meant to be magic but to reveal his unique sharing in God's creative and liberating power for the world.

Mark does not set out to tell what actually happened in the storm. What he does tell us is that the power of God was made visible that day in the lives of Jesus and his disciples when they nearly drowned together in the lake.

The experience by the disciples of such extraordinary power in Jesus leaves them terrified and wondering who Jesus really is and what he brings to the world.

1 They came to the other side of the sea, to the country of the Gerasenes. 2 And when he had stepped out of the boat, immediately a man out of the tombs with an unclean spirit met him. 3 He lived among the tombs; and no one could restrain him any more, even with a chain; 4 for he had often been restrained with shackles and chains, but the chains he wrenched apart, and the shackles he broke in pieces; and no one had the strength to subdue him. 5 Night and day among the tombs and on the mountains he was always howling and bruising himself with stones. 6 When he saw Jesus from a distance, he ran and bowed down before him; 7 and he shouted at the top of his voice, he said, 'What have you to do with me, Jesus, Son of the Most High God? I adjure you by God, do not torment me.' 8 For he had said to him, 'Come out of the man, you unclean spirit!' 9 Then Jesus asked him, 'What is your name?' He replied, 'My name is Legion; for we are many.' 10 He begged him earnestly not to send them out of the country.

11 Now there on the hillside a great herd of swine was feeding; 12 and the unclean spirits begged him, 'Send us to the swine, let us enter them.' 13 So he gave them permission. And the unclean spirits came out and entered the swine; and the herd, numbering about two thousand, rushed down the steep bank into the sea, and were drowned in the sea.

14 The swineherds ran off and told it in the city and in the country. Then people came to see what it was that had happened. 15 They came to Jesus, and saw the demoniac sitting there, clothed and in his right mind, the very man who had had the legion; and they were afraid. 16 Those who had seen what had happened to the demoniac and to the swine reported it. 17 Then they began to beg Jesus to leave their neighbourhood. 18 As he was getting into the boat, the man who had been possessed by demons begged him that he might be with him. 19 But Jesus refused, and said to him, 'Go home to your friends, and tell them how much the Lord has done for you, and what mercy he has shown you.' 20 And he went away and began to proclaim in the Decapolis how much Jesus had done for him; and everyone was amazed.

III/9. The healing of a madman

On the other side of the lake lived Gentile Gerasenes. The town of Gerasa was about 50 kilometres south-east of the lake. A violent madman of great strength appeared out of the tombs. Madness in the time of Jesus was popularly believed to be from an evil spirit controlling a person.

Jesus asks the name of the demon. In the Bible, to know the name of anyone is already to have power over them. The madman is broken and torn by many demons and names himself 'legion', an army division of six thousand or more soldiers.

Despite their great number, the demons know they are the presence of a greater power in Jesus. They ask to be allowed to go and live in a herd of pigs grazing close by.

Jesus frees the man from the power of the demons, but his power is so great that he frees the surrounding place also, for the pigs go rushing madly into the sea and drown themselves. Evil eventually destroys life.

The Jewish disciples of Jesus saw pigs as unclean and their drowning a good thing. The Gerasenes, however, ask Jesus to leave. They understand nothing but their loss of so many pigs.

The drama which began with the rage of the madman and the power in Jesus, then shifted to the pigs and later to the people of that place, now returns to focus on Jesus and the former madman sitting peacefully and restored to his full humanity.

The man asks to go with Jesus, but his discipleship will be of another kind. Jesus sends him among his own people to tell them of the great work of power God has done in him. Instead, he tells others what Jesus did for him, and all who heard him began to wonder. Wonder can be the beginning of true faith!

21 When Jesus had crossed again in the boat to the other side, a great crowd gathered around him; and he was by the sea.

22 Then one of the leaders of the synagogue named Jairus came and, when he saw him, fell at his feet 23 and begged him repeatedly, 'My little daughter is at the point of death. Come and lay your hands on her, so that she may be made well, and live.' 24 So he went with him. And a large crowd followed him and pressed in on him.

25 Now there was a woman who had been suffering from hemorrhages for twelve years. 26 She had endured much under many physicians, and had spent all that she had; and was no better but rather grew worse. 27 She had heard about Jesus, and came up behind him in the crowd and touched his cloak, 28 for she said, 'If I but touch his clothes, I will be made well.' 29 Immediately her hemorrhage stopped; and she felt in her body that she was healed of her disease.

30 Immediately aware that power had gone forth from him, Jesus turned about in the crowd and said, 'Who touched my clothes?' 31 And his disciples said to him, 'You see the crowd pressing in on you; how can you say, "Who touched me?"' 32 He looked all around to see who had done it.

33 But the woman, knowing what had happened to her, came in fear and trembling and fell down before him, and told him the whole truth. 34 He said to her, 'Daughter, your faith has made you well; go in peace, and be healed of your disease.'

Starters

1. Stand on the shore of the lake and watch Jesus arrive in the boat. Look at him as he steps from the boat and watch the crowd gather.

2. Single out Jairus and the suffering woman. Follow in your imagination their different ways of coming to Jesus and notice what you feel.

III/10. Jesus heals a woman

In this passage Mark uses his 'sandwich' technique of placing one story within another. The story of Jairus and his young daughter at the point of death is begun, but before it is ended, a second story is told of an unnamed woman in the crowd whom Jesus heals of her sickness.

In this way Mark links two events closely and invites us to read one in the light of the other.

Both stories are of cures that no human power could work. In different ways they each reveal the greatness of the power that is made present to people in Jesus, a power so divine and yet so available to people with faith in God.

Our attention is drawn to an important man in the great crowd that gathers around Jesus after his arrival in the boat. He is one of the leaders of the synagogue in that place, yet he comes to Jesus in great humility to beg him to come and touch his dying daughter. At once Jesus goes with him followed by the crowd.

Then our attention is shifted to a woman in the crowd. She has been hemorrhaging for twelve years, perhaps since her puberty, which would make her a woman in her early twenties. With such an illness, marriage would be impossible, and by the Jewish blood taboo she should not appear in public. Much less should she touch another!

Secretly she comes to Jesus and touches him. Jesus feels power going out of him and the woman feels healing.

Being human, he needs to ask who has been cured by the divine power passing from him. He does not accuse the woman for breaking the law, but praises her for the faith that drew divine power from him.

35 *While he was still speaking, some people came from the leader's house to say, 'Your daughter is dead. Why trouble the teacher any further?'* 36 *But overhearing what they said, Jesus said to the leader of the synagogue, 'Do not fear, only believe.'*

37 *He allowed no one to follow him except Peter, James and John the brother of James.*

38 *When they came to the house of the leader of the synagogue, he saw a commotion, people weeping and wailing loudly.*

39 *When he had entered, he said to them, 'Why do you make a commotion and weep? The child is not dead but sleeping.'* 40 *And they laughed at him. Then he put them all outside, and took the child's father and mother and those who were with him, and went in where the child was.*

41 *He took her by the hand he said to her, 'Talitha cum,' which means, 'Little girl, get up!'* 42 *And immediately the girl got up and began to walk (she was twelve years of age). At this they were overcome with amazement.*

43 *He strictly ordered them that no one should know this, and told them to give her something to eat.*

Starters

1. *Try to feel what Jesus may have felt as the story unfolds in the brief words of Mark.*

2. *Compare the touch that cured the young girl with the touch that cured the woman in the crowd.*

III/11. Jesus raises a young girl

This passage continues and concludes the story about Jairus and his young daughter at the point of death. Here, as we noticed earlier, Mark uses his 'sandwich' technique by placing within this first story a second story about the sick woman in the crowd, who touches his clothes. In this way Mark intentionally makes a close link between the two narratives.

In both stories someone is given new life by contact with the divine power brought by Jesus. The older woman touches Jesus, the younger woman is touched by Jesus. In both situations human efforts have failed, but Jesus brings new life, a sure sign that God's power is being revealed in him.

Notice how dramatically Mark tells the story, preparing us for the climax of the restoration of the young girl to life. Jesus brings only three of his disciples with him. He sees the commotion from outside. When he enters the house, he shuts out all but the family and his disciples. For Jesus, death is only a sleeping.

Despair has overtaken the house of Jairus when Jesus arrives. He tells Jairus to keep trusting in God. Then he goes into the house and stops the noise of traditional mourning. His work needs faith not only in himself but in those around. He goes to where the dead girl lies and restores life to her, and all wonder.

The episode ends with Jesus asking them to tell no one outside the little group of those who showed faith, and to give food to the girl.

For Mark's first readers, as for us today, the request of Jesus to give the girl food calls up images of the eucharist which sustains all Christians in the new life given them by Christ in baptism.

Mark 6:1-6a

¹*He left that place and came to his hometown; and his disciples followed him.*

²*On the sabbath he began to teach in the synagogue, and many who heard him were astounded. They said, 'Where did this man get all this? What is this wisdom that has been given to him? What deeds of power are being done by his hands!*

³*'Is not this the carpenter, the son of Mary and brother of James and Joses and Judas and Simon, and are not his sisters here with us?' And they took offense at him.*

⁴*Then Jesus said to them, 'Prophets are not without honor, except in their hometown, and among their own kin, and in their own house.'*

⁵*And he could do no deed of power there, except that he laid his hands on a few sick people and cured them.*

⁶ᵃ*And he was amazed at their unbelief.*

Starters

1. *Try to enter into the atmosphere among the people of Nazareth when Jesus returns to be with them. Reflect on why they become hostile.*

2. *Ponder the effect of lack of faith in those around Jesus upon the power of the gospel which he brings to the world.*

III/12. The miracle that wasn't

For a fifth and final miracle we travel with Jesus and his disciples from the lakeside up the Galilean hills to his native place. From elsewhere (1:9,24) we know this is Nazareth.

Jesus goes to the synagogue on the Sabbath. His return home is more than a private or nostalgic visit. He is offering his own people the gospel of the kingdom of God. There is a depth in what he says which the people sense and they are confused. What is the source of his teaching, for they saw him grow up in their town? What is the nature of his wisdom, for it comes with a divine power to heal and re-create?

The wonder of the people turns to resistance. They reject his invitation to believe in the new gospel he brings. They take offence that he should challenge them so deeply. They are scandalised by the ordinariness of one who has recently lived among them, it seems, as a carpenter.

They know his mother Mary and his cousin-brothers, as the catholic tradition understands them, and his sisters also. James, Joses, Jude and Simon are apparently not among the twelve, although some of the twelve have similar names.

The point of the story came at the end. Jesus appears surprised that he can do no real work of power in his home town, because, it seems, they were lacking faith. The human disappointment in Jesus must have been real, but the proverb quoted by him about the prophet underlines the need for faith around a prophet, if he is to do the great works of a prophet.

Jesus can do no real work of power there that brings them conversion and freedom of heart. He merely lays his hands upon a few sick persons who come to him and heals them.

69

IV

JESUS IN HIS MISSION

Mark 6:6b — 8:30

Mark 6:6b-13

6b *Then he went about among the villages teaching.*

7 *He called the twelve and began to send them out two by two, and gave them authority over the unclean spirits.*

8 *He ordered them to take nothing for their journey except a staff; no bread, no bag, no money in their belts;* **9** *but to wear sandals and not to put on two tunics.*

10 *He said to them, 'Wherever you enter a house, stay there until you leave the place.*

11 *'If any place will not welcome you and they refuse to hear you, as you leave, shake off the dust that is on your feet as a testimony against them.'*

12 *So they went out and proclaimed that all should repent.*

13 *They cast out many demons, and anointed with oil many who were sick and cured them.*

Starters

1. *Reflect on the simplicity of lifestyle Jesus asks and consider how much I seek this as a way to experience God's power in my life.*

2. *Consider what power Jesus shares with the twelve. Try to enter into something of their feelings as they set out.*

IV/1. The disciples sent into mission

A brief summary passage (6b) opens a new part of Mark's Gospel, where he has gathered stories of missionary journeys of Jesus and his disciples beyond the familiar synagogues and towns of the lakeside.

After the failure in the synagogue at Nazareth, Jesus no longer teaches in the synagogues and towns but continues his teaching moving among the villages of the countryside. He calls the twelve, whom he chose earlier (3:14), and sends them two by two on a mission, asking of them the same mobility and flexibility. In Jewish law two are necessary for a valid witness.

They are sent to share in the mission of Jesus to reveal the kingdom of God in the world. The authority to do this, which Jesus has from God, he gives to them. It is an authority that goes beyond teaching in words and shows itself in a new power over evil spirits which oppress people, to free people from sicknesses and to turn human hearts towards God.

Like John the baptiser, the disciples do not explicitly proclaim the kingdom in words. In Mark's Gospel Jesus alone does this.

They are to be mobile, symbolised by the travelling staff, and they are to be flexible, living in simplicity without provision for food, money or extra clothing, trusting in the providence of God. Like Jesus they are to remain in a place as long as they are made welcome. The gesture of wiping the feet before leaving was a sign among the Jews of separating oneself from a people who lacked true faith in God.

The six pairs of disciples leave Jesus and go off to witness to the coming of the kingdom of God into the world. They call for a radical turning to God, they drive out demons and they anoint the sick with oil.

14King Herod heard of it, for Jesus' name had become known. Some were saying, 'John the baptiser has been raised from the dead; and for this reason these powers are at work in him.' 15But others said, 'It is Elijah.' And others said, 'It is a prophet, like one of the prophets of old.' 16But when Herod heard of it, he said, 'John, whom I beheaded, has been raised.'

17For Herod himself had sent men who arrested John, bound him, and put him in prison on account of Herodias, his brother Philip's wife, because Herod had married her. 18For John had been telling Herod, 'It is not lawful for you to have your brother's wife.'

19And Herodias had a grudge against him, and wanted to kill him. But she could not, 20for Herod feared John, knowing that he was a righteous and holy man, and protected him. When he heard him, he was greatly perplexed; and yet he liked to listen to him.

21But an opportunity came when Herod on his birthday gave a banquet for his courtiers and officers and for the leaders of Galilee. 22When the daughter Herodias came in and danced, she pleased Herod and his guests; and the king said to the girl, 'Ask me for whatever you wish, and I will give it.' 23And he solemnly swore to her, 'Whatever you ask me, I will give you, even half of my kingdom.' 24She went out, and said to her mother, 'What should I ask for?' She replied, 'The head of John the baptiser.' 25Immediately she rushed back to the king and requested, 'I want you to give me at once the head of John the Baptist on a platter.' 26The king was deeply grieved; yet out of regard for his oaths and for the guests, he did not want to refuse her. 27Immediately the king sent a soldier of the guard with orders to bring John's head. He went out and beheaded him in the prison, 28brought his head on a platter, and gave it to the girl. Then the girl gave it to her mother. 29When his disciples heard about it, they came and took his body, and laid it in a tomb.

IV/2. The lonely death of John

Between the departure of the twelve on their mission (6:7-14) and their return (6:30) Mark has inserted the story of the death of John the baptiser, as he called him. It is the only story in Mark's Gospel that is not directly about Jesus.

The placing of the story of John's death at the only time in Mark's Gospel when Jesus is separated from his disciples suggests a meaning. John's death by Herod points to Jesus' own death at the hands of the powerful.

It points also to what discipleship means. During the sufferings and death of Jesus his disciples are separated from him, not by a mission but by cowardly unfaithfulness.

This Herod was Herod Antipas, a son of Herod the Great in the story of Jesus' birth, who was the tetrarch of Galilee and Perea from 4 BC until 39 AD. His fear appears to be a superstitious dread that John the baptiser whom he had killed was alive again.

Those around Herod offer him all kinds of misinformation telling him that Jesus was not John but Elijah, or another of the old prophets.

When compared with the story in the first century Jewish historian Josephus, there are differences in the way Mark tells the story of John's death. Mark presents the death of John as a foretelling of the death of Jesus himself and a model for all disciples of Jesus.

The forthrightness of John in rebuking Herod when he was doing what was against the law of God parallels the daring of Jesus when he proclaims the gospel in Jerusalem and confronts the powerful leaders there. John is betrayed by Herodias as Jesus is by Judas.

John dies in loneliness as Jesus dies deserted by the twelve. The disciples of John come to bury his body, but who come to bury the body of Jesus?

30 *The apostles gathered around Jesus, and told him all that they had done and taught.* 31 *He said to them, 'Come away to a deserted place all by yourselves and rest a while.' For many were coming and going, and they had no leisure even to eat.* 32 *And they went away in the boat to a deserted place by themselves.*

33 *Now many saw them going and recognised them, and they hurried there on foot from all the towns and arrived ahead of them.* 34 *As he went ashore, he saw a great crowd; and he had compassion for them, because they were like sheep without a shepherd; and he began to teach them many things.*

35 *When it grew late, his disciples came to him and said, 'This is a deserted place, and the hour is now very late;* 36 *send them away so that they may go into the surrounding country and villages and buy something for themselves to eat.'* 37 *But he answered them, 'You give them something to eat.' They said to him, 'Are we to go and buy two hundred denarii worth of bread, and give it to them to eat?'* 38 *And he said to them, 'How many loaves have you? Go and see.' When they had found out, they said, 'Five, and two fish.'* 39 *Then he ordered them to get all the people to sit down in groups on the green grass.* 40 *So they sat down in groups of hundreds and of fifties.* 41 *Taking the five loaves and the two fish, he looked up to heaven, and blessed and broke the loaves, and gave them to his disciples to set before the people; and he divided the two fish among them all.* 42 *And all ate and were filled;* 43 *and they took up twelve baskets full of broken pieces and of the fish.* 44 *Those who had eaten the loaves numbered five thousand men.*

Starters

1. *Compare the compassion of Jesus for the people with the readiness of his disciples to send them away.*
2. *Consider the ways that this sharing of such little food among so many symbolises the mystery of the eucharist.*

IV/3. Sharing food with five thousand

When the disciples return from their mission and tell Jesus all they did and taught, he invites them to come and rest in a quiet place by the lake.

This plan is frustrated when a crowd of people hurry along the shore of the lake and are there to welcome him and his disciples when they arrive. Like a good shepherd in the prophecy of Ezekiel (Ezek 34:11-16), Jesus feels compassion for them and begins to teach them.

After he has nourished the people with his teaching in that desert place, Jesus concludes by sharing food with them. He tells his disciples not to send the people away to get food, but to give them food from the little they have.

There are Old Testament comparisons: Moses fed the wandering Israelites in the desert with birds and manna (Ex 16:11-21), and Elisha fed a hundred people with twenty barley loaves and still had food left over (2 Kings 4:42-44).

By sharing food Jesus generates a sense of unity among that huge crowd as they sit down on the green grass and eat together. When he takes the bread and fish, blesses God, breaks the loaves and gives them to his disciples to give the people, the link with what he did at the meal before he died is clear (14:22). There is plenty of food left over, one large basketful for each of the twelve to take and share with still more people!

Unlike the miraculous healings by Jesus, Mark mentions no surprise or wonder among the disciples or the crowd. Whether in fact Jesus miraculously produced more bread and fish or whether the sharing of the little food he and his disciples had with them stirred others to do the same, is left to our imagination.

Mark shows that Jesus brings wholeness of life. He feeds the crowd from the little which his disciples had.

45 *Immediately he made his disciples get into the boat and go ahead to the other side, to Bethsaida, while he dismissed the crowd.*

46 *After saying farewell to them, he went up on the mountain to pray.*

47 *When evening came, the boat was out on the sea, and he was alone on the land.*

48 *When he saw that they were straining at the oars against an adverse wind, he came towards them early in the morning, walking on the sea. He intended to pass them by.* 49 *But when they saw him walking on the sea, they thought it was a ghost and cried out;* 50 *for they all saw him and were terrified. But immediately he spoke to them and said, 'Take heart, it is I; do not be afraid.'*

51 *Then he got into the boat with them and the wind ceased. And they were utterly astounded,* 52 *for they did not understand about the loaves, but their hearts were hardened.*

Starters

1. *Imagine and contrast what Jesus felt in his prayer on the mountain with what his disciples felt as they rowed against the wind.*

2. *Sense the feelings of the disciples in the boat rowing all night across the lake, especially what they felt when they saw Jesus.*

IV/4. Jesus comes to struggling disciples

After the meal at the lakeside, Jesus makes his disciples move to Bethsaida. Bethsaida, east of the Jordan's opening into Lake Galilee, may have been for Mark, a symbol of Gentile country. Then Jesus goes alone into the hills by the lake to pray.

Jesus alone in prayer on the shore and the disciples apart from him out on the lake, rowing their boat against the wind, are dramatically contrasted. It is not clear where Jesus is when he sees his disciples struggling. Nor is it clear how he comes to them. The phrase 'walking on the sea' could also mean 'walking by the sea'.

Mark takes it in the former sense, suggesting God's creative control over nature in the Old Testament, symbolised by his walking on the waters of the sea and his sudden comings and goings (Job 9:5-12). They must have been rowing all night when Jesus came to them early in the morning.

The fear of the disciples and their cry to Jesus for help recall the earlier storm of wind on the lake and the terror they felt at that time (4:35-41). As he did then, Jesus quickly rescues them. When he gets into the boat and is again with them, the wind drops. The desperate situation of the disciples when separated from Jesus and their security when he is with them are sharply contrasted.

The terror of the disciples after the first storm on the lake is now replaced by a hardness of heart, or lack of faith, that makes them like the Pharisees (3:5). They do not yet understand Jesus and what he brings to the world.

The wholeness of life he offers them and through them all the people is still hidden from them. The real meaning of the sharing of their little food with the crowd is not yet understood by them.

53 *When they had crossed over, they came to land at Gennesaret and moored the boat.*

54 *When they got out of the boat, people at once recognised him,* 55 *and rushed about that whole region and began to bring the sick on mats to wherever they heard he was.*

56 *And wherever he went, into villages or cities or farms, they laid the sick in the marketplaces, and begged him that they might touch even the fringe of his cloak; and all who touched it were healed.*

Starters

1. *Feel something of the neediness of the people crowding around Jesus and the power that was in him.*

2. *Reflect a little on the readiness of Jesus to live close to the needs of others and the confusion that comes from this.*

IV/5. Summary: Jesus among people

The journeys of Jesus and his disciples in the fourth part of Mark's Gospel (6:6b — 8:30) continue in this episode. After the dramatic all-night crossing over the lake from where they had shared their food with the huge crowd, they landed at Gennesaret. This is a small coastal plane on the shore of the lake, west of Bethsaida, the place for which the disciples had first set out.

Mark presents these verses as a summary passage describing the kind of welcome Jesus was accustomed to receive from the people in Galilee at that time.

In our imagination we can try to visualise the people crowding to Jesus from all sides. We can feel the confusion as relatives and friends rush to carry their sick and disabled ones to wherever Jesus is.

The sick ask to touch even the fringe of his clothes. Those who do this are cured, just as in an earlier episode the sick woman had been when she secretly touched with faith the clothing of Jesus (5:27-28).

The image of Jesus that Mark presents is of one constantly on the move, passing through different villages, towns and countrysides. He is close to people, among them as one of them. He is not described as a teacher but as one who heals all the sick who are brought to him. He makes himself available to as many as want to come to him. His disciples travel with him always. They see all he does as silent observers.

In this part of his Gospel Mark describes missionary travels of Jesus, first towards the Jews of Israel (6:6b — 7:23), it seems, and then later, out into the towns and country of the Gentiles (7:24 — 8:30).

In each place the sick and those who suffer other evils are freed and made whole by the power of this missionary Jesus, always with his disciples moving onward.

1 Now when the Pharisees and some of the scribes who had come from Jerusalem gathered around him, 2 they noticed that some of his disciples were eating with defiled hands, that is, without washing them.

3 (For the Pharisees, and all the Jews, do not eat unless they thoroughly wash their hands, thus observing the tradition of the elders; 4 and they do not eat anything from the market place, unless they wash it; and there are also many other traditions that they observe, the washing of cups, pots and bronze kettles.)

5 So the Pharisees and the scribes asked him, 'Why do your disciples not live according to the tradition of the elders, but eat with defiled hands?'

6 He said to them, 'Isaiah prophesied rightly about you hypocrites, as it is written, 'This people honours me with their lips, but their hearts are far from me; 7 in vain do they worship me, teaching human precepts as doctrines.' 8 You abandon the commandment of God, and hold to human tradition.'

9 Then he said to them, 'You have a fine way of rejecting the commandment of God in order to keep your tradition! 10 For Moses said, "Honour your father and your mother"; and, "Whosoever speaks evil of father or mother must surely die." 11 But you say that anyone tells father or mother, "Whatever support you might have had from me is Corban" (that is, an offering to God) — 12 then you no longer permit doing anything for a father or mother, 13 thus making void the word of God through your tradition that you have handed on. And you do many things like this.'

Starters

1. *What does Jesus teach about the relation of some religious practices to the word of God?*
2. *Reflect on the attitude of Jesus that is manifested in his teaching on the practices of the Pharisees and scribes.*

IV/6. Danger from false interpretations

One of the great obstacles to mobility and flexibility in the mission of the church during the first decades of Christianity were the interpretations of the Jewish law which resulted in long lists of community practices and ritual observances which many of the first Christians as Jews brought with them. It is probably why Mark introduces this passage and the next into this fourth part of his Gospel (6:6b — 8:30), which describes missionary journeys of Jesus with his disciples. Both passages describe the attitude of Jesus towards certain Jewish religious practices.

When the local Pharisees with learned scribes from Jerusalem saw some of his disciples eating without first ritually purifying themselves, they confront Jesus. They had many rules for ritual washings of the body before eating and for the washing of pots, cups and dishes. All these things were to be done according to the 'Halakah', or Jewish oral law, considered by the Pharisees to bind as the 'Torah', or God's law itself.

In reply Jesus first quotes the prophet Isaiah, who warns: You honour God with your lips but not with your hearts; your worship is worthless, your doctrines are only human rules (Is 29:13)! Jesus tells the Pharisees they have put aside God's law and clung to human rules (6-8)!

The second reply of Jesus picks out the Jewish practice of Corban, or consecrating things to God. Human relationships are abused by declaring things consecrated to God. Jesus shows how this becomes a way of putting aside God's law by denying one's natural duties and relations to others. Even the special relation of children to parents was left aside in the name of God. Such rules and practices empty the true meaning of God's law through Moses (9-13).

Jesus goes to human needs when he teaches what God's law means. Religious practices are not meant to destroy genuine freedom and a true concern for others.

14 Then he called the crowd again and said to them, 'Listen to me, all of you, and understand: 15 there is nothing outside a person that by going in can defile, but the things that come out are what defile.'

17 When he had left the crowd and left the people, his disciples asked him about the parable.

18 He said to them, 'Then do you also fail to understand? Do you not see that whatever goes into a person from outside cannot defile, 19 since it enters, not the heart but the stomach, and goes out into the sewer?' (Thus he declared all foods clean.)

20 And he said, 'It is what comes out of a person that defiles.

21 'For it is from within, from the human heart, that evil intentions come: fornication, theft, murder, 22 adultery, avarice, wickedness, deceit, licentiousness, envy, slander, pride, folly.

23 'All these evil things come from within, and they defile a person.'

Starters

1. *What are some things in my life that I can honestly admit to be evil?*

2. *Consider some of the things in my life that nourish my fidelity to God.*

3. *Look up lists of evils like the one in this passage in other parts of the New Testament (Rom 1:29-31, Gal 5:19-21, 1 Pet 4:3).*

IV/7. Need for interiority

In this passage, Jesus calls the people around him and teaches what religious practice is meant to be and what constitutes uncleanness or impurity in God's eyes. The teaching of Jesus is given in two ways: first, there is a teaching for all (14-15), second, a deeper teaching for the disciples (17-23).

To the crowd Jesus tells a brief parable. A person can never be made unclean by something which comes from the outside. It is what comes from within a person that brings uncleanness. The source of true purity and religion that unites one with God is inside a person not outside. Merely external circumstances or situations can never separate a person from God. Only personal choices can do this.

For the disciples, in the privacy of a house, an early Christian symbol of the church, Jesus explains his teaching. He first points to the lack of understanding of his teaching among the disciples, as he has already done before (4:13, 6:52). Then he gives the earthy parable of food passing into and out of the human body (18b-19).

By this comparison he clarifies for the disciples his emphasis that a right interior disposition, and not merely exterior religious practices, constitute in God's eyes genuine purity. Jesus twice repeats to his disciples what he has already taught the people. Real evil can come to a person only from within one's own heart (20 and 23).

The teaching of Jesus on the need for interiority in religious practices ends with a systematically arranged list of different kinds of evil that can flow from interior uncleanness or disorder in the human heart. In Mark's list, there are twelve evils, six in the plural indicating particular actions: sexual vices, thefts, murders, adulteries, acts of coveting, and wickednesses; and six in the singular describing habitual attitudes: deceitfulness, wantonness, envy, slander, arrogance, and folly or lack of moral judgment.

24 *From there he set out and went away to the region of Tyre. He entered a house and did not want anyone to know he was there. Yet he could not escape notice,* 25 *but a woman whose little daughter had an unclean spirit, immediately heard about him, and she came and bowed down at his feet.*

26 *Now the woman was a Gentile, of Syrophoenician origin. She begged him to cast the demon out of her daughter.*

27 *He said to her, 'Let the children be fed first, for it is not fair to take the children's food and throw it to the dogs.'*

28 *But she answered him, 'Sir, even the dogs under the table eat the children's crumbs.'*

29 *Then he said to her, 'For saying that, you may go — the demon has left your daughter.'*

30 *So she went home, found the child lying on the bed, and the demon gone.*

Starters

1. *What do the sincerity and the feelings in this woman say to you?*

2. *Try to enter into the feelings of Jesus as this woman argued with him.*

IV/8. The healing at Tyre

Jesus withdraws from the opposition to his mission in Galilee into the Gentile countryside around the coastal cities of Tyre and Sidon to the north of Israel. He goes there quietly, not in a public way. Yet, as Mark says to his readers, Jesus could not be hidden for long.

A Greek-speaking woman, a Phoenician from Syria, comes to seek him out. Agonised by grief she falls down at the feet of Jesus in the house where he was. Her little daughter is possessed by evil and she begs Jesus to free her from this demon.

The conversation between the woman and Jesus shows the characters of both. There is the woman's love for her absent daughter, her earnest faith in the power of Jesus to heal, and her confident hope that he will drive out the evil in her.

In Jesus there is a strange reluctance at first to show his power in this Gentile world. He admires the woman's persistence and recognises a genuine faith in her towards the power that was in him to free people from evil.

We are given a glimpse of his attractive simplicity when he humbly accepts that the woman has bested him in the argument. In his human consciousness is there a dawning awareness that God sends him also to the Gentiles outside Israel?

Through the genuine faith in God which he recognises in this Greek woman, Jesus is able to free the daughter from the evil that possessed her, even though she herself is absent. The woman questions no more.

Trusting that through Jesus she has been blessed by God and her daughter freed from evil, she quietly goes off to her home. There she finds her child cured, lying calmly in her bed. The power in Jesus frees from evil wherever he finds persons of true faith in God.

Mark 7:31-37

³¹ *Then he returned from the region of Tyre, and went by way of Sidon towards the Sea of Galilee, in the region of the Decapolis.*

³² *They brought to him a deaf man who had an impediment in his speech; and they begged him to lay his hand on him.*

³³ *He took him aside in private, away from the crowd, and put his fingers into his ears, and he spat and touched his tongue.*

³⁴ *Then looking up to heaven, he sighed and said to him, 'Ephphatha,' that is, 'Be opened.'*

³⁵ *And immediately his ears were opened, his tongue was released, and he spoke plainly.*

³⁶ *Then Jesus ordered them to tell no one; but the more he ordered them, the more zealously they proclaimed it.*

³⁷ *They were astonished beyond measure, saying, 'He has done everything well; he even makes the deaf to hear and the dumb to speak.'*

Starters

1. *Imagine that you are in the crowd watching when Jesus heals this man. What do you see and hear and feel?*

2. *Imagine that you yourself are the one touched and healed by Jesus. What do you feel?*

IV/9. A healing in the Decapolis

Jesus continues his journey into the Decapolis. To go from Tyre south-east to the Lake of Galilee by first going north to Sidon, then east to the Decapolis, then west to the lake is hardly a direct route. Mark's aim, however, is not strictly geographical detail, but to portray Jesus as missionary, one who goes with his disciples to people in different places, even outside Israel, as they once came to him (3:8). For Mark, it is in Galilee and nearby places that the gospel is first announced and believed (1:14-15). Only later does Jesus go south to Jerusalem.

The people bring a deaf and dumb man, one unable to speak properly, and they ask Jesus to touch him and heal him. The situation of early Christians, where the community brings individuals to be touched by Jesus in life-giving actions of the church, may be the context which Mark has in mind.

Jesus takes the man apart from the unbelieving crowd and does the healing in private. Such a context, away from surrounding unbelief, invites our faith to contemplate devoutly how Jesus frees this man from evil.

With his fingers he touches the man's deaf ears. With spittle from his mouth he touches the man's twisted tongue. He looks up to God and sighs with sorrow, or even anger (1:41), for the man's condition. He speaks an Aramaic word 'Ephphatha'.

The human actions of Jesus manifest divine power. The prophet Isaiah says God would heal the deaf and the dumb when he came to free his people (Is 35:4-5). The crowd is astonished 'beyond measure', the strongest statement of surprise at a miracle in all of Mark's Gospel.

A really deaf person is anyone who does not hear the gospel and believe in God. A really dumb person is one who does not proclaim the gospel of God and share it with others!

Mark 8:1-10

1 In those days, when there was again a great crowd without anything to eat, he called his disciples and said to them, 2 'I have compassion for the crowd, because they have been with me now for three days and have nothing to eat. 3 If I send them away hungry to their homes, they will faint on the way — and some of them have come from a great distance.'

4 His disciples replied, 'How can one feed these people with bread here in the desert?'

5 He asked them, 'How many loaves do you have?' They said, 'Seven.'

6 Then he ordered the crowd to sit down on the ground; and he took the seven loaves, and having given thanks he broke them and gave them to his disciples to distribute; and they distributed them to the crowd.

7 They had also a few small fish; and having blessed them, he ordered that these too should be distributed.

8 They ate and were filled; and they took up the broken pieces left over, seven baskets full.

9 Now there were about four thousand people. And he sent them away.

10 And immediately he got into the boat with his disciples and went to the district of Dalmanutha.

Starters

1. *Does this passage say anything to me about the link between the eucharist and a Christian community or the Christian mission?*

2. *How would I feel if I were one of the disciples and were asked by Jesus to share my food with others?*

IV/10. Feeding four thousand for the way

Mark's second version of the loaves and fish, like the first (6:30-44), concerns a huge crowd of people, mentions the large quantity of food left over, and takes place in the desert. Again, the central Christian action of the eucharist is implied by the use of the three key phrases: took, gave thanks over, and broke the bread.

Both stories conclude with a journey across the lake. The context in Mark also suggests that while the first meal was in Galilee by the lakeside, this second meal was in a neighbouring Gentile region, where people also need the food that the Messiah brings (7:27-28).

There are differences too. Five thousand eat from five loaves and two fish, and twelve baskets are filled with food left over in the first story. In the second story, four thousand people eat from seven loaves and a few fish, and seven baskets are filled with the food that remained.

In the first story the compassion of Jesus was underlined by his readiness to teach the people, but in this story his compassion is shown by his desire to give them food to eat.

This second meal in the desert draws our attention to the need of this food for people who journey with Jesus in mission. The people have been with him for three days. Without this food people will become faint-hearted along the way.

An allusion to the eucharist is more pronounced, since there is no mention of the few fish until after the people have eaten the bread. This highlights bread, part of the central symbol of the eucharist from the earliest Christian times.

The seven large baskets, each of which could be large enough to hold a person, suggest that here is something for all the Gentile world, since the number seven in the Bible usually suggests completeness and universality.

11 The Pharisees came and began to argue with him, asking him for a sign from heaven, to test him.

12 And he sighed deeply in his spirit and said, 'Why does this generation ask for a sign? Truly I say to you, no sign will be given to this generation.'

13 And he left them, and getting into the boat again, he went across to the other side.

Starters

1. *Reflect for a while on what kind of signs I would expect God to give to reveal divine power in the world.*

2. *Try to enter into the interior feeling of Jesus which causes his deep sigh.*

IV/11. No signs for Pharisees

After the second meal in a desert place, Jesus went with his disciples to the district of Dalmanutha (8:10). The geographical location of this place is unknown, but Mark seems to understand it to be on the western shore of the lake, across from the place where the crowd was fed the second time, apparently in the Decapolis on the eastern side of the lake.

We find opposition to Jesus resumed when the Pharisees come and start to argue with him again. The lesson of the meal in the desert that Jesus can nourish people with new life is lost on them. These Jewish religious leaders in Galilee seek signs that convince them that Jesus is from God.

The word 'sign', used three times in this short passage, is not Mark's usual word for a work of Jesus. Mark understands the works of Jesus not so much as signs of something hidden but as works of divine power coming into the world to free people from evils.

There are signs that convince and signs that witness. The former prove beyond all doubt, the latter invite. While the former operate no matter what a person's interior attitude may be, the latter can witness to happenings only where there is an interior readiness to see. The Pharisees asked for the former, but Jesus offered the latter.

Jesus responds to the lack of faith in the Pharisees with a deep sigh. Mark has mentioned the emotions of Jesus before (1:41, 3:5, 6:34). The phrase 'Truly (literally 'Amen'), I say to you', is used by Mark only in the sayings of Jesus to emphasise an important teaching.

In a symbolic gesture, Jesus leaves the Pharisees and gets back into the boat for another crossing of the lake, towards Bethsaida on the eastern shore, the place to where Jesus has earlier told his disciples to go ahead of him (6:45).

14 Now the disciples had forgotten to bring any bread; and they had only one loaf with them in the boat.

15 And he cautioned them, saying, 'Watch out — beware of the yeast of the Pharisees and the yeast of Herod.'

16 They said to one another, 'It is because we have no bread.'

17 And becoming aware of it, Jesus said to them, 'Why are you talking about having no bread? Do you still not perceive or understand? Are your hearts hardened?

18 Do you have eyes, and fail to see? Do you have ears, and fail to hear? And do you not remember?

19 When I broke the five loaves for the five thousand, how many baskets full of broken pieces did you collect?' They said to him, 'Twelve.'

20 And the seven for the four thousand, how many baskets full of broken pieces did you collect?' And they said to him, 'Seven.'

21 Then he said to them, 'Do you not yet understand?'

Starters

1. *Look up some other times when the disciples failed to understand Jesus: 4:13, 40, 6:52, 7:18. Can I find times like this in my own life?*

2. *Spend some time letting each of the questions of Jesus sink into my heart. Savour any feelings that stir within me.*

IV/12. Dangers from religion and politics

It is not only the Pharisees who fail to understand (8:11-13). The disciples too, who are with Jesus always in his journeys and observe all he does and says, do not yet understand who Jesus is and what is the power he brings into the world.

In this episode Jesus points to the lack of understanding in his disciples (8:17-21). They fail to grasp the real meaning of his words and actions, as they travel with him in his journeys. The disciples need to guard within themselves against the same evil motives and dispositions, or 'leaven', which Jesus sees in the Pharisees and the Herodians.

The leaven of the Pharisees is contentment with their limited interpretations of God's law and their narrow religious practices, and so they fail to see the power of God in the works and words of Jesus. The leaven of the Herodians is probably their abuse of political power, failing to respect the dignity of people and the justice due to others.

The dispositions and the motivation for their lives, which Jesus desires for his disciples, will be very different, neither trusting in limited views of God's law and religious practice, as the Pharisees do, nor becoming slaves to selfish ambitious for political power, like the Herodians.

When Jesus crossed the lake after the first meal in the desert, there was an argument with the Pharisees (7:1-23) and a discussion about bread (7:24-30). Likewise, when he crosses the lake after the second meal, there is again an argument with the Pharisees (8:11-13) and now in this passage a discussion about bread (8:14-21).

Jesus challenges his uncomprehending disciples to a deeper level of faith in his person with one question after another. The bread that they really need is what Jesus offers in all he does and says. It is the power of God to give life and freedom to people.

²² *They came to Bethsaida. Some people brought a blind man to him and begged him to touch him.*

²³ *He took the blind man by the hand, and led him out of the village; and when he had put saliva on his eyes and laid his hands on him, he asked him, 'Can you see anything?'*

²⁴ *And the man looked up and said, 'I can see people, but they look like trees, walking.'*

²⁵ *Then Jesus laid his hands on his eyes again; and he looked intently and his sight was restored, and he saw everything clearly.*

²⁶ *Then he sent him away to his home, saying, 'Do not even go into the village.'*

Starters

1. *Notice the three different times that Jesus touched the blind man.*

2. *Try to share the feelings of the blind man after he felt the first touch of Jesus, then the second, and finally the third touch.*

IV/13. The blind man at Bethsaida

Only now do Jesus and his disciples arrive at Bethsaida (6:45), a village in the Gentile country situated on the northeastern side of the lake where the Jordan river enters.

The people ask Jesus to touch a blind man. He does this, but secretly and in three stages, putting saliva on his eyes, laying hands on him, and laying hands on his eyes again. Only after the third touch does the blind man see clearly.

By this story at Bethsaida Mark leads us towards the conclusion of the missionary journeys of Jesus (6:6b—8:30), and prepares us for the central episode of his Gospel, which immediately follows, on the true identity of Jesus.

The healing of a deaf and dumb man (7:31-37) reminds us that to share as disciples in the mission of Jesus we need to hear what Jesus really says and share it with others. The healing of this blind man tells us that true disciples need to see the divine power that Jesus brings to the world, and see this not in a confused way but clearly.

Mark uses this story of the blind man to introduce the theme of blindness in the disciples, as Jesus forms them with difficulty in his way, a formation that comes to a climax with the dramatic cure of another blind man, Bartimaeus at Jericho (10:46-52).

The healing of the blind man is a strange story because Jesus cures his blindness in three stages. The apparent lack of power in Jesus may be why the other Gospels omit this story.

The blind man's two stages of seeing, however, prepare us for the two ways of naming Jesus in the following passage (8:27-30). The three touches by Jesus anticipate his repeated efforts to enlighten his disciples and form them as disciples by three passion prophecies in the next part of Mark's Gospel (8:31—10:52).

Mark 8:27-30

27 Jesus went on with his disciples to the villages of Caesarea Philippi; and on the way he asked his disciples, 'Who do people say I am?'

28 And they answered him, 'John the Baptist; and others, Elijah; and still others, one of the prophets.'

29 He asked them, 'But who do you say that I am?' Peter answered him, 'You are the Messiah.'

30 And he sternly ordered them not to tell anyone about him.

Starters

1. How much can I feel within myself that Christ is a significant person in my life? The most significant?

2. Compare the first and second touches of Jesus on the blind man in the last story with the two replies to his question here.

IV/14. Who am I for you?

We have here a first climax in Mark's Gospel, which was said at the beginning to be about Jesus as Christ and Son of God. Here he is named the Christ or Messiah. Only after his death will he be publicly named Son of God (15:39).

Jesus is still outside Israel, travelling among the villages to the north near Caesarea Philippi where the Jordan river rises from the mountains. The 'way', used by Mark here and several times in the next part of his Gospel, can mean not only to the physical roadway, but may also symbolise the 'way' Jesus is teaching his disciples to walk as true disciples, the theme of the next part of his Gospel (8:30—10:52).

Jesus first asks what outsiders, people who are not disciples, say about him. Various answers are given which identify him with great figures from Israel's past, for like the blind man they do not see clearly yet. Then Jesus asks his disciples, 'But who do you say that I am?'

Earlier, Jesus silenced the demons who named him (1:34, 3:12) and also the people whom he cured (7:36, 8:26). His disciples asked among themselves in astonishment and in terror, who is this man (4:25)? Now Jesus himself asks his disciples to name him, as he asks each of us, not from any book knowledge but from an experience of being touched by him in one's own life.

Peter, like the blind man when he sees clearly, names him the Messiah, which means Christ, the one anointed by God for the divine task of revealing his power to Israel. Peter is thinking of the popular expectation of a worldly and political Messiah. At the same time it may be Peter's best word to identify the most wonderful person he has ever met.

This episode serves as a bridge passage which concludes the first half of Mark's Gospel and begins the second.

V

JESUS FORMS HIS DISCIPLES

Mark 8:31 — 10:52

Mark 8:31-33

31 Then he began to teach them that the Son of man must undergo great suffering, and be rejected by the elders, the chief priests, and the scribes, and be killed, and after three days rise again.

32 He said all this quite openly. And Peter took him aside and began to rebuke him.

33 But turning and looking at his disciples, he rebuked Peter and said, 'Get behind me, Satan! For you are setting your mind not on divine things but on human things.'

Starters

1. *Imagine that Christ says to me what he said to Peter. From my own experience of Jesus, what name would I give to him?*

2. *Am I ready to read this fifth part of Mark's Gospel (8:31—10:52) with the eyes and ears of a disciple being formed in the 'way' of Jesus?*

V/1. The first passion prophecy

This and the following episode are the core of Mark's Gospel. Peter sees Jesus as the Messiah, but he still has to learn what kind of Messiah Jesus really is, and the way he will show himself as God's Son. Peter and the disciples need, like the blind man, to be touched repeatedly by Jesus to see clearly.

The teaching which Jesus now begins to give his disciples is about the kind of Messiah he will be and is a formation in the way he wants his disciples to follow. Until now Jesus has astonished and challenged his disciples, but in this episode and the next he begins to prepare them to imitate him.

The teaching of Jesus is grouped by Mark around three brief summaries of his future suffering and his vindication by God. These summaries are generally known as passion prophecies, but they are just as much resurrection prophecies too.

After this first passion prophecy, just as after two later passion prophecies, it is clear that the disciples fail to grasp what Jesus says (8:32b-33). He describes himself as one who will suffer and be rejected as of no value by the political, religious and intellectual leaders of the people. He will finally be put to death in disgrace, but soon rise again.

This rising again has no impact on the disciples. Their attention is fixed on the first part of his prophecy. How can the life of the Messiah of God end in failure and disgrace?

Peter takes Jesus aside and rebukes him. How can Jesus expect to keep his disciples when he speaks like that! Jesus, looking around and seeing his disciples, in return rebukes Peter. He calls him a Satan, one who opposes the plans of God. Peter's way of thinking is merely human. He still needs to be formed as a true disciple of Jesus.

103

34 He called the crowd with his disciples, and said to them, 'If any want to become my followers, let them deny themselves and take up their cross and follow me.

35 'For those who want to save their life will lose it, and those who lose their life for my sake, and for the sake of the gospel, will save it.

36 'For what will it profit them to gain the whole world and forfeit their life?

37 'Indeed, what can they give in return for their life?

38 'Those who are ashamed of me and of my words in this adulterous and sinful generation, of them will the Son of Man also be ashamed, when he comes in the glory of his Father with the holy angels.'

1 And he said to them, 'Truly I tell you, there are some standing here who will not taste death until they see that the kingdom of God has come with power.'

Starters

1. *Do I feel within myself a true desire to give myself to this 'way' of being a disciple of Jesus?*

2. *Do I feel a willingness, when this 'way' may call for it, to put a loss before profit, or social rejection before social acceptability?*

V/2. A way of the cross

Jesus calls both the crowd and his disciples, an indication that something important is to be said. He has spoken openly of his eventual failure but final vindication, and Peter has failed to grasp his meaning. We are at the centre of Mark's Gospel.

Jesus corrects Peter's misunderstanding and gives a new teaching. His way is a way of the cross, that means losing one's life to find it again in a new way (8:34-35). Other sayings, probably spoken by Jesus at different times, are placed here by Mark (8:35—9:1).

The call of Jesus to deny oneself is much more than a call to do penance. It is a call to a radical turning from self-centredness to God-centredness, which is possible only through the gospel-power of God himself. It is that *'metanoia'* or personal conversion which Jesus can effect through the gospel he brings (1:15).

To carry one's cross is more than a patient acceptance of suffering. The cross was an instrument of terrible torture unto death. Yet it meant more. It was the sign of rejection by society. The cross was a sign of social unacceptability, a sign that one's way of living, one's values in life, were not acceptable to the rest of society.

To be a disciple of Jesus means putting other things, one's comfort, one's reputation, one's business or social interests in the second place.

A disciple who fears to accept this value system but lives for things like prestige, power, property or pleasure, things good in themselves but not the purpose of life, will not be recognised by Jesus as his own, neither now nor in the future, when the kingdom of God comes in full power. To find one's true self, Jesus teaches, we need to have the person we think we are taken from us and discover the real person we can become.

Mark 9:2-13

2 *Six days later Jesus took with him Peter and James and John, and led them up a high mountain apart, by themselves. And he was transfigured before them,* 3 *and his clothes became dazzling white, such as no one on earth could bleach them.*

4 *And there appeared to them Elijah with Moses who were talking with Jesus.*

5 *Then Peter said to Jesus, 'Rabbi, it is good for us to be here; let us make three dwellings, one for you, one for Moses, and one for Elijah.'* 6 *He did not know what to say, for they were terrified.*

7 *Then a cloud overshadowed them, and from the cloud there came a voice, 'This is my Son, the Beloved; listen to him!'*

8 *Suddenly when they looked around, they saw no one with them any more, but only Jesus.*

9 *As they were coming down the mountain, he ordered them to tell no one about what they had seen, until after the Son of Man had risen from the dead.* 10 *So they kept the matter to themselves, questioning what this rising from the dead could mean.*

11 *Then they asked him, 'Why do the scribes say that Elijah must come first?'*

12 *He said to them, 'Elijah is indeed coming first to restore all things. How then is it written about the Son of Man, that he is to go through many sufferings and be treated with contempt?* 13 *But I tell you that Elijah has come, and they did to him whatever they pleased, as it is written about him.'*

Starters

1. *Imagine myself on the mountain with the three disciples. The disciples felt terror. What would I feel?*
2. *Consider how Jesus shares this experience with the disciples after he spoke openly of his future suffering and disgraceful death (8:31 — 9:1).*

V/3. The transfiguration of Jesus

This episode happens six days after Jesus taught his way as a way of the cross. Six, one less than seven, a symbol of completeness, suggests the incompleteness of the revelation of Jesus to his disciples. He spoke of his way as a way of disgrace and rejection.

Now on a mountain apart Jesus shares with his three closest disciples the glory and acceptance which he has from God. For a second time (1:11), Jesus is shown as he really is, the Son of God. The four times when Jesus is identified as Son of God, here and at the Jordan river by God, and later by himself in his passion and finally by a Roman centurion after his death, are like the four great 'pillars' of Mark's Gospel.

Elijah, the prophet, nine centuries before Christ, and Moses, the Old Testament liberator of Israel twelve centuries before Christ, appear beside him. Both were prophets who suffered, and there was a Jewish belief that at death both Elijah (2 Kings 2:11-12) and Moses (Deut 34:5-6) were taken bodily into heaven.

Peter sees Jesus, Moses and Elijah as equals. He has not yet discovered the superior destiny of Jesus. The cloud, or Jewish 'Shekinah', signifying divine presence and communication, envelops them. They hear the voice of God, not spoken only to Jesus as it was at the Jordan river, but also to the three disciples.

Suddenly, Jesus stands alone with them as his ordinary self. Coming down the mountain, he tells them to keep hidden what they saw until his rising from death, when this revelation will become clear to all his disciples.

The Pharisees taught that Elijah would return before God restored divine glory to Israel and transformed human lives (Mal 4:5). Jesus says that Elijah has come already in John the baptiser who was treated so badly, a reminder of what will be done to the Messiah himself.

14 When they came to the disciples, they saw a great crowd around them, and some scribes arguing with them. 15 When the whole crowd saw him, they were immediately overcome with awe, and they ran forward to greet him. 16 He asked them, 'What are you arguing about with them?' 17 Someone from the crowd answered him, 'Teacher, I brought you my son: he has a spirit that makes him unable to speak; 18 and whenever it seizes him, it dashes him down; and he foams and grinds his teeth and becomes rigid; and I asked your disciples to cast it out, and they could not do so.' 19 He answered them, 'You faithless generation, how much longer must I be among you? How much longer must I put up with you? Bring him to me.' 20 And they brought the boy to him. When the spirit saw him, immediately it convulsed the boy, and he fell down on the ground and rolled about, foaming at the mouth. 21 Jesus asked the father, 'How long has this been happening to him?' And he said, 'From childhood. 22 It has often cast him into the fire and into the water, to destroy him; but if you are able to do anything, have pity on us and help us.' 23 Jesus said to him, 'If you are able! — All things can be done for the one who believes.' 24 Immediately the father of the child cried out, 'I believe; help my unbelief!'

25 When Jesus saw that a crowd came running together, he rebuked the unclean spirit, saying to it, 'You spirit that keeps this boy from speaking and hearing, I command you, come out of him, and never enter him again.' 26 After crying out and convulsing him terribly, it came out, and the boy was like a corpse, so that most of them said, 'He is dead.' 27 But Jesus took him by the hand and lifted him up, and he was able to stand.

28 When he had entered the house, his disciples asked him privately, 'Why could we not cast it out?' 29 He said to them, 'This kind can come out only through prayer.'

V/4. Jesus heals an epileptic boy

This story, after the revelation on the mountain of the real identity of Jesus as Messiah, shows again the power of Jesus to free from evil, but also the powerlessness of his disciples.

They do not yet fully know Jesus or the way he goes. Perhaps there is a parallel with the revelation to Jesus by God at the Jordan river (1:9-11) and his struggle with Satan that followed in the desert (1:12-13).

The sickness of the boy, the anguish of his desperate father, the lack of faith in the disciples, the scribes, the crowd, and in the father himself is described. Mark helps us to feel the inner pain of Jesus as he senses the lack of faith around him.

God is so ready to heal human brokenness and reveal his power over evil, but human channels are lacking. The burden falls on Jesus alone, himself supremely the man of faith and responsiveness to what God does in the world.

Jesus seeks to foster the little faith which the father of the boy, a symbol of the disciples themselves, already has. Ponder the reply of Jesus to the father, 'What is this if-you-can? Everything is possible for one who has faith!' Jesus speaks to his disciples as well as to the father.

Jesus wants to free the boy from the sickness before too many curious people gather around him. Emphasising the need for faith in the boy's father, he drives the evil from the boy with such power that all think the boy has died.

When the disciples, who earlier had power to drive out demons (6:7), are alone with Jesus, they ask him why they were unable to drive out this demon. This kind of evil, Jesus tells them, can be driven out only by a faith that is nourished in prayer, in the way his own faith was.

Mark 9:30-34

30 They went on from there and passed through Galilee. He did not want anyone to know it; 31 for he was teaching his disciples, saying to them, 'The Son of Man is to be betrayed into human hands, and they will kill him; and three days after being killed, he will rise again.'

32 But they did not understand what he was saying and were afraid to ask him.

33 Then they came to Capernaum; and when he was in the house he asked them, 'What were you arguing about on the way?'

34 But they were silent, for on the way they had argued with one another who was the greatest.

Starters

1. Pause a moment and honestly search my heart to see how much fear remains in my own attitude towards Jesus or towards God.

2. Notice how the disciples for a second time misunderstand what Jesus has said to them about his 'way'.

V/5. A second passion prophecy

For a second time, as they are travelling quietly through Galilee, Jesus begins to speak to his disciples of terrible sufferings for himself in the future. It seems, that writing in the seventies, Mark adds more specific detail from hindsight of these future sufferings than Jesus at the time actually spoke.

Jesus with a firm trust in his final vindication by God may have done no more than warn his disciples in a general kind of manner of the likely dishonourable death awaiting him, and the failure of his mission by merely human standards.

As after the first passion prophecy (8:32-33), the disciples fail to understand what Jesus says to them about his future, and they are too frightened to question him. They still have much to learn about the mission of Jesus and a lot of growing to do in their relations with him.

When they arrive home in Capernaum, Jesus asks what they were discussing on the way. They keep silent. So far are they from understanding what Jesus has just been saying to them that they had been discussing with one another who was greatest among them.

Mark contrasts starkly the failure of the disciples to understand with the effort of Jesus to teach them about his way. The 'way' used twice here (9:33-34) means not only the roadway to Capernaum, but points also to the way of true discipleship into which Jesus tries to lead them.

Are we also unable to bring our questionings to Christ in an honest and trustful faith? Do we also need to look into the dispositions of our own hearts and ask ourselves with honesty how much do we grasp what it means to be a true disciple of Jesus? Is our faith in the divine power of Christ, whom we follow, large enough to make us ready to walk faithfully his 'way'?

35 He sat down, called the twelve and said to them, 'Whoever wants to be first must be last of all and servant of all.'

36 Then he took a little child and put it among them; and taking it in his arms, he said to them, 37 'Whoever welcomes one such child in my name welcomes me, and whoever welcomes me welcomes not me but the one who sent me.'

38 John said to him, 'Teacher, we saw someone casting out demons in your name, and we tried to stop him, because he was not following us.'

39 But Jesus said, 'Do not stop him; for no one who does a deed of power in my name will be able soon afterward to speak evil of me.

40 Whoever is not against us is for us.

41 For truly I tell you, whoever gives you a cup of water to drink because you bear the name of Christ will by no means lose the reward.

Starters

1. Notice the attitude of Jesus towards the child and one outside the group. How tolerant and welcoming am I towards people like these?

2. Consider how Jesus is asking his disciples to be less exclusive and less triumphal in their following of him.

V/6. A way of little ones

After the first passion prophecy, when Peter failed to understand what he said, Jesus called his disciples to give them teaching about his way. Then it was a teaching about a way of the cross (8:34-35). Here it is a teaching of a way for little ones.

Jesus seats himself and calls around him his disciples, as the master about to give an important teaching. For a second time, he teaches them something new about his 'way' that corrects their misunderstanding. His way is a way for 'little ones'.

This means finding a new position for oneself as leader in a community — the last place! Two incidents recalled from the life of Jesus are added to illustrate this teaching.

The first is a story of the little child whom Jesus stands in the midst of his disciples and tenderly holds in his arms (9:36-37). Whoever receives, that is, listens, to the little ones among the disciples of Jesus receives Jesus as the Messiah, and whoever receives the Messiah receives God, the one who sends the Messiah.

The second story is of a person who drives out demons in the name of the Messiah but is not a member of their own group of disciples (9:38-41). The outsider is doing a work of divine power in the name of Jesus, which freeing human lives from evil always is.

Such a one cannot be acting against the mission of the Messiah and God's plan for the world. The disciples of Jesus will not always be the ones to initiate the good that God seeks to accomplish in the world.

The last place is not a popular place. It is the position of one at the call of others. The last is one whose life is largely controlled by others. A little one relies on the care of others to survive. A little one is vulnerable to all.

Mark 9:42-50

42 'If any of you put a stumbling block before one of these little ones who believe in me, it would be better for you if a great millstone were hung round your neck and you were thrown into the sea.

43 If your hand causes you to stumble, cut it off; it is better for you to enter life maimed than to have two hands and to go to hell, to the unquenchable fire.

45 And if your foot causes you to stumble, cut it off; it is better for you to enter life lame than to have two feet and to be thrown into hell.

47 And if your eye causes you to stumble, tear it out; it is better for you to enter the kingdom of God with one eye than to have two eyes and to be thrown into hell, 48 where their worm never dies, and the fire is never quenched.

49 For every one will be salted with fire.

50 Salt is good; but if salt has lost its saltiness, how can you season it? Have salt in yourselves, and be at peace with one another.'

Starters

1. Think a little of times I may have harmed the faith of others by what I did or failed to do.

2. Consider how much my faith gives a special 'taste' to my day-to-day living as a Christian, that is, one who follows Jesus as the Christ.

V/7. Five sayings of Jesus on scandal

This is the first of five passages (9:42—10:31), which Mark has loosely arranged together, containing episodes that say something about the 'way' for disciples as a way for little ones (9:35). After the first passion prophecy and the new teaching about the way as a way of the cross (8:34-35), there were also added appropriate teachings and stories (8:36—9:29).

The five sayings of Jesus, which Mark places in this passage, are linked by the theme of scandal towards little ones. Little ones symbolise the true followers of Jesus, made little in the eyes of the world and vulnerable towards others around them by the depth of their faith in God and their wholehearted commitment to the way of Jesus.

Scandal here is understood not in its modern sense of sharing gossip or harming another's good name, but in the biblical sense of putting obstacles and hindrances to true faith in another or in oneself. Anyone who harms the faith of another deserves the worst of penalties (9:42).

The teaching of Jesus puts dramatically before his disciples, in images that would certainly shock them, their central need to humble themselves as little ones before God and God's plan for the world. It would be better to lose a hand, a foot or an eye than to lose their faith in God. Gehenna, originally, it seems, a rubbish-dump continually burning outside Jerusalem, became a Jewish symbol of hell as a place of personal destruction and separation from God the life-giver and saviour.

The saying that everyone will be salted by fire (9:49) could mean that the faith of a true disciple is tested by suffering.

The next verse is clearer. Salt without taste is useless. Faith that does not touch one's life is equally useless. The final words of Jesus point to a close connection between faith in God and harmony in our lives together.

1 He left that place and went to the region of Judea and beyond the Jordan. And crowds again gathered around him: and, as was his custom, he again taught them.

2 Some Pharisees came, and to test him they asked, 'Is it lawful for a man to divorce his wife?'

3 He answered them, 'What did Moses command you?'

4 They said, 'Moses allowed a man to write a certificate of dismissal and to divorce her.'

5 But Jesus said to them, 'Because of your hardness of heart he wrote you this commandment. 6 But from the beginning of creation, 'God made them male and female.' 7 'For this reason a man shall leave his father and mother and be joined to his wife, 8 and the two shall become one flesh.' So they are no longer two, but one flesh. 9 Therefore what God has joined together, let no one separate.'

10 Then in the house the disciples asked him again about this matter.

11 He said to them, 'Whoever divorces his wife and marries another commits adultery against her; 12 and if she divorces her husband and marries another, she commits adultery.'

Starters

1. *Pray to Jesus for a few moments in a spirit of faith for a true understanding of his teaching on marriage.*

2. *Try to look at your own marriage or another's as Jesus would see it.*

V/8. The teaching of Jesus on marriage

By placing this passage here, with teachings of Jesus about discipleship as a way for little ones, Mark seems to consider as little ones women in Jewish marriages, and all those, women or men, who try to live a lifelong fidelity in marriage.

Jesus is travelling again, this time in the towns of Judea and on the other side of the Jordan river. Crowds gather around him again, and he teaches them. Some Pharisees question him in a hostile manner about his attitude towards divorce.

'Is it lawful for a man to divorce his wife?' they bluntly ask him. Jesus replies that Moses allowed divorce of a wife (Deut 24:1) only because of 'their hardness of heart', which means their lack of understanding, rather than a lack of feeling. God's plan is for a man or woman to marry for life, Jesus explains, and he quotes from the Book of Genesis (1:27, 2:24).

In this way Jesus, gives his disciples who follow his 'way' a clear ideal of marriage as a lifelong commitment to each other. Lifelong fidelity to each other in marriage by disciples becomes part of their response in faith to God's powerful action in the world. Living as disciples, trying like Jesus to walk his 'way' as little ones before God's power, can be the source of a fidelity in marriage that will last.

Although among the Gentiles divorce was generally allowed to both men and women, for the Jews at the time of Jesus, adultery was an injustice which a woman committed against her husband or a man committed against another man through that other man's wife.

The injustice towards a woman was not considered. For Jesus, divorce and remarriage among his disciples, by either a man or a woman, points to a lack of faith in God, an evil like the infidelity of adultery itself.

117

13 People were bringing little children to him in order that he might touch them; and the disciples spoke sternly to them.

14 But when Jesus saw this, he was indignant and said to them, 'Let the little children come to me; do not stop them; for it is to such as these that the kingdom of God belongs.

15 'Truly I say to you, whoever does not receive the kingdom of God as a little child will never enter it.'

16 And he took them up in his arms, laid his hands on them, and blessed them.

Starters

1. *Can I see why this passage was used in the second century by supporters of baptism for infants?*

2. *Let me pray for the gift of becoming little enough to feel wonder always towards all that God does so marvellously in the world.*

V/9. Jesus blesses little children

The well-known scene of Jesus blessing the children is placed here by Mark, maybe because children are so obviously the little ones who all are called to be who follow the 'way' of Jesus.

There is a difference in being childish and being child-like. Childishness is selfishness, a refusal to grow up and become part of the world, not its centre. To be childlike is something else, and it is to this attitude Jesus calls his disciples. It is a necessary condition to belong, to receive, or to enter the kingdom of God, the favourite phrase of Jesus for the gospel.

Jesus welcomes the intrusion of the children. Contrast the unwelcoming attitude of his disciples. He is angry when the disciples rebuff them. Within this human affection for children we sense something of the depth of his mysterious sensitivity for the kingdom of God. When he takes the children into his arms and blesses them, placing his hands upon them, we can see how human and affectionate Jesus is, but we see also in him a sign of God's power coming into the world.

An important teaching of Jesus, recognisable by the characteristic phrase used by him to give emphasis, 'Truly (Amen), I say to you', stands at the centre of the passage. One must receive the kingdom of God like a little child to enter it.

Children naturally wonder at things. They are readily taken out of themselves and become absorbed in whatever is happening. The gift of wonder, natural to a child, usually lessens in adults. The disciples of Jesus, on the contrary, are called to grow in wonder at the ever-new things of God as they grow in years. Surely this is the root of the simplicity one senses in Jesus himself. It makes cynicism or disillusionment impossible for disciples who follow the 'way' of the little ones.

Mark 10:17-22

17 As he was setting out on a journey, a man ran up and knelt before him, and asked him, 'Good Teacher, what must I do to inherit eternal life?'

18 Jesus said to him, 'Why do you call me good? No one is good but God alone.

19 'You know the commandments: "You shall not murder; You shall not commit adultery; You shall not steal; You shall not bear false witness; You shall not defraud; Honour your father and mother."'

20 He said to him, 'Teacher, I have kept all these since my youth.'

21 Jesus, looking at him, loved him and said, 'You lack one thing; go, sell what you own, and give the money to the poor, and you will have treasure in heaven; then come, follow me.'

22 When he heard this, he was shocked and he went away grieving, for he had many possessions.

Starters

1. *The treasure in heaven of which Jesus speaks is God. Where is what I love most in life — my treasure?*

2. *Consider how I become like this rich man when I try to live as if I can be a follower of Jesus as the Christ by my unaided human efforts.*

V/10. Jesus calls a rich man

This story begins by reminding us that Jesus is still travelling. A rich man runs up to Jesus and kneels before him to ask, 'Good Teacher, what must I do to inherit eternal life?' The law of Moses already taught this, but the man wants something more. What more must he do?

Jesus first challenges the man's idea of goodness. Why is anyone good? Does it come from something one must do or should do, earned by a kind of legal right? Or is it, as Jesus experiences, something that comes from God as gift?

Jesus does not pursue that subtle challenge. Instead, he repeats the commandments of God which Moses gave the people. The man has kept all these since he was young. He has evidently lived a good life by doing all he felt he must do.

Why does Jesus look at the rich man and love him with affection? Is it the goodness he admires in the man? The love of Jesus for the man is better linked not to what he has just said to Jesus, but to what Jesus will say to him.

The love of Jesus, as God's love, is a beginning rather than an end. It is divine energy and inspiration empowering a greater good rather than a recognition or reward for good already done.

The man needs to experience not only God's commands, but God's enabling love. He needs to be centred on the 'treasure in heaven'. All the rich man understands seems to be the hard words about giving away all his riches. He looks down and sadly turns away from Jesus.

Perhaps if this man had kept looking at Jesus and been little enough to let Jesus love him, he may have found in the face of Jesus the divine power enabling him to do what humanly he could never do.

23 Then Jesus looked around and said to his disciples, 'How hard it will be for those who have wealth to enter the kingdom of God!'

24 And the disciples were perplexed at these words. But Jesus said to them again, 'Children, how hard it is to enter the kingdom of God!

25 'It is easier for a camel to go through the eye of a needle than for someone who is rich to enter the kingdom of God.'

26 They were greatly astounded and said to one another, 'Then who can be saved?'

27 Jesus looked at them and said, 'For mortals it is impossible, but not for God; for God all things are possible.'

28 Peter began to say to him, 'Look, we have left everything and followed you.'

29 Jesus said, 'Truly I tell you, there is no one who has left house or brothers or sisters or mother or father or children or fields, for my sake and for the sake of the gospel, 30 who will not receive a hundredfold now in this age — houses, brothers and sisters, mothers and children, and fields with persecutions — and in the age to come eternal life.

31 'But many who are first will be last, and the last will be first.'

Starters

1. Notice how strongly, by an exaggerated illustration, Jesus puts the difficulty for wealthy people to welcome the gospel.

2. How much can I really accept this teaching of Jesus on wealth?

V/11. The teaching of Jesus on wealth

Jesus shocks his disciples when he tells them it is hard for the wealthy to enter the kingdom of God, to experience God's power coming into the world. Like most Jews of that time they see wealth as a clear sign of God's blessing.

The disciples are even more amazed when Jesus says with tenderness towards them how hard it is for anyone to enter the kingdom of God. His comparison of a camel trying to pass through the eye of a needle shocks again.

Jesus exaggerates to emphasise his teaching. He implies the difficulty, even human impossibility, for the wealthy to have real contact through faith with the kingdom of God. Yet what may be humanly impossible can still be possible for God.

As the rich man in the previous story failed to understand, eternal life, which is really another word for the kingdom of God, does not come simply from doing the right thing, doing what we should do. It is always God's free gift.

Peter characteristically reminds Jesus that he and the other disciples left all to follow him. Jesus emphasises, with 'Truly (Amen) I say to you', that those who have left any person or possession for his sake, and the gospel he brings, will receive a hundredfold blessing of God. They receive this now by their experience of community and the things they share, paradoxically with persecution too, Mark adds, and in the future by sharing eternal life, the life of the eternal God.

Mark ends this fifth episode of a group of five (9:35 — 10:31) connected with the teaching of Jesus about the need for his disciples to be little ones with words that summarise and shock. The last and little ones now will be revealed later as the ones who are the first and truly great in the way God sees things.

Mark 10:32-40

32 They were on the road, going up to Jerusalem, and Jesus was walking ahead of them; they were amazed, and those who followed were afraid. He took the twelve aside again and began to tell them what was to happen to him, 33 saying, 'See, we are going up to Jerusalem, and the Son of Man will be handed over to the chief priests and the scribes, and they will condemn him to death; then they will hand him over to the Gentiles; 34 they will mock him, and spit upon him, and flog him, and kill him; and after three days he will rise again.'

35 James and John, the sons of Zebedee, came forward to him and said to him, 'Teacher, we want you to do for us whatever we ask of you.'

36 And he said to them, 'What is it you want me to do for you?'

37 And they said to him, 'Grant us to sit, one at your right hand and one at your left, in your glory.'

38 But Jesus said to them, 'You do not know what you are asking. Are you able to drink the cup that I drink, or to be baptised with the baptism that I am baptised with?'

39 They replied, 'We are able.' Then Jesus said to them, 'The cup that I drink you will drink; and with the baptism with which I am baptised, you will be baptised; 40 but to sit at my right hand or at my left is not mine to grant, but it is for those for whom it has been prepared.'

Starters

1. What does this incident teach about the way along which Jesus wants to lead his disciples?

2. Recall an example you know of the effect of selfish ambition in a group. What feelings does it stir in you now?

V/12. A third passion prophecy

The third foretelling by Jesus of his sufferings, death and final vindication is again within the setting of a journey. It is explicitly said this time that he is on his way to Jerusalem. He walks in front of his disciples, but they follow, shocked and fearful.

As in the other two prophecies of his passion (8:31 and 9:31), Jesus describes himself in the third person as the Son of Man, a mysterious title which he alone uses of himself. It underlines the human solidarity Jesus shares with his disciples, yet points to a mystery in him which stirs questions about his true identity.

This prophecy is more detailed and more terrible than the two earlier ones. Mark probably adds details from hindsight at the time he wrote, but it is clear once again that Jesus expects shameful treatment, fearsome sufferings and condemnation to death from the leaders of his own people and from the foreign occupying power, before he is finally vindicated by God.

The disciples again fail to grasp what Jesus is trying to share with them, as they twice did earlier (8:32 and 9:32). We even find the two brothers, James and John, coming to Jesus to ask for themselves the top places beside him, when he comes to rule in the worldly glory and secular power they still expect for him as the Messiah.

Jesus challenges them by asking them were they able to drink the cup of suffering he would drink, or to be immersed in the baptism of a passion and death with which he would be baptised.

In their ignorance and arrogance the two think they can. Jesus assures them that if they faithfully follow him as disciples they will certainly experience this cup and this baptism. The places in the glory of the kingdom, however, when the kingdom is fully revealed at some future time, are only for God to give.

Mark 10:41-45

41 When the ten heard this, they began to be angry with James and John.

42 So Jesus called them to him and said to them, 'You know that among the Gentiles those whom they recognise as their rulers lord it over them, and their great ones are tyrants over them.

43 But it is not so among you; but whoever wishes to become great among you must be your servant, 44 and whoever wishes to be first among you must be slave of all.

45 For the Son of Man came not to be served but to serve, and to give his life a ransom for many.'

Starters

1. *Try to feel the demanding simplicity that Jesus asks and lived himself in forming his disciples.*

2. *What do I feel are things in my life from which I need to be ransomed or freed by the power that Jesus has brought to the world?*

3. *Once again, look up some of the places where Jesus names himself Son of Man: 2:10, 28, 8:31, 38, 9:9, 12, 31, 10:33, 45, 13:26, 14:21, 41, 62.*

V/13. A way of servants and slaves

When the ambition of James and John angers the other disciples, Jesus for the third time calls them all to give them a new and corrective teaching about the 'way' they are to follow as his disciples (8:34-35 and 9:35).

Jesus has first taught them that his 'way' was 'a way of the cross', by which a disciple finds God as the new centre of one's life (8:34). Secondly, he taught that it is 'a way of little ones', by which a disciple seeks in the last place a new position in life (9:35). Now thirdly, Jesus teaches them that his way is a 'way of servants and slaves', by which a disciple discovers by a humble service of others a new function in life (10:43-44).

The behaviour of the great and powerful in secular society is not to be the norm among the disciples. For them greatness is to be measured not by power and control but by a humble, even menial service.

Disciples of Jesus are to be distinguished by a readiness to be servants and even slaves for one another. Such an ideal of leadership by service will be possible in the disciples only when they welcome within themselves the same power of God that works in Jesus.

Among people who live without faith in God, Jesus told his disciples, those who seem to rule, although it is always God who really rules, dominate and control the lives of others. The same can be true today, where political, industrial and commercial leaders often dominate and control the lives of ordinary people. Even religious leaders can dominate others in the manner which Jesus describes as characteristic of the unbelieving Gentiles of his day, people without true faith in God.

Jesus is among his disciples as one who does not demand to be served, but who serves even to the giving of his life for them.

Mark 10:46-52

46 *They came to Jericho. As he and his disciples and a large crowd were leaving Jericho, Bartimaeus, son of Timaeus, a blind beggar, was sitting by the roadside.*

47 *When he heard that it was Jesus of Nazareth, he began to shout out and say, 'Jesus, Son of David, have mercy on me!'*

48 *Many sternly ordered him to be quiet, but he cried out even more loudly, 'Son of David, have mercy on me!'*

49 *Jesus stood still and said, 'Call him here.' And they called the blind man, saying to him, 'Take heart; get up, he is calling you.'*

50 *So throwing off his cloak, he sprang up and came to Jesus.*

51 *Then Jesus said to him, 'What do you want me to do for you?' The blind man said to him, 'My Teacher, let me see again.'*

52 *Jesus said to him, 'Go; your faith has made you well.' Immediately he received his sight and followed him on the way.*

Starters

1. *Let me imagine myself in Bartimaeus sitting beside the way, apart from the others and seeing nothing, but hearing.*

2. *Imagine Jesus looking at me, when I do not see him, and let me hear him ask me, 'What do you want me to do for you?'.*

V/14. Blind Bartimaeus at Jericho

The story of Bartimeaus concludes the teaching of Jesus about service of others (10:32-52). Jesus serves this blind man, begging beside the roadway, by freeing him from his blindness.

The giving of sight to the blind Bartimaeus also concludes the fifth part of Mark's Gospel, where Jesus has been forming his disciples in his 'way' (8:31 — 10:52). With the earlier healing of the blind man at Bethsaida (8:22-26), the healing of Bartimaeus forms a 'frame' for the whole of this part, where Jesus tries, unsuccessfully, to enlighten the blindness of his disciples.

As Jesus leaves Jericho on his journey up to Jerusalem, his disciples and a large crowd of people follow him. At the side of the roadway sits the blind Bartimaeus begging. He is apart from the disciples and the others, and unable to see. He hears Jesus of Nazareth is there and begins to shout for mercy without knowing exactly where to shout. He calls Jesus Son of David, a title for the expected Messiah. The crowd try to silence him, but the more they try, the more he shouts.

Jesus stops and asks them to call him. Bartimaeus eagerly jumps to his feet, throws away the cloak, which likely he has spread on the ground before him to receive alms, and runs to Jesus. Notice how the disciples and others are drawn to help, once Jesus begins to act.

It is clear what Bartimaeus wants. Nonetheless, Jesus asks him to speak it out. He stands in his blindness before Jesus, whom he cannot see, with nothing but his human need to be healed. Through the faith of Bartimaeus Jesus gives him sight.

Though told to go, Bartimaeus does not go. His eyes have begun to see. No longer does he sit beside the 'way' as an outsider. He follows Jesus as a disciple joyfully, maybe with dancing, along the 'way' up the slope to Jerusalem.

VI

JESUS COMES TO JERUSALEM

Mark 11:1 – 13:37

1 When they were approaching Jerusalem, at Bethphage and Bethany, near the Mount of Olives, he sent two of his disciples 2 and said to them, 'Go into the village ahead of you, and immediately as you enter it, you will find tied there a colt that has never been ridden; untie it and bring it.

3 'If anyone says to you, "Why are you doing this?" just say this, "The Lord needs it and will send it back here immediately." '

4 They went away and found a colt tied near a door, outside in the street. As they were untying it, 5 some of the bystanders said to them, 'What are you doing, untying the colt?' 6 They told them what Jesus had said; and they allowed them to take it.

7 Then they brought the colt to Jesus and threw their cloaks on it; and he sat on it. 8 Many people spread their cloaks on the road, and others spread leafy branches that they had cut from the fields.

9 Then those who went ahead and those who followed were shouting, 'Hosanna! Blessed is the one who comes in the name of the Lord! 10 Blessed is the coming kingdom of our ancestor David! Hosanna in the highest heaven!'

11 Then he entered Jerusalem and went into the temple; and when he had looked around at everything, as it was already late, he went out to Bethany with the twelve.

Starters

1. *Try to feel something of what Jesus must have felt as he rode down the Mount of Olives into Jerusalem.*

2. *Can I with the disciples give praise and thanks for the way God is coming into my life at this time?*

VI/1. Jesus enters Jerusalem

Jesus draws near to Jerusalem at Bethphage and Bethany to enter the city from the Mount of Olives to the east, since he has come from Jericho near the Jordan river. He is about to begin in Jerusalem what in Mark's Gospel is a brief ministry (11:1 — 13:37).

The Prophecy of Zechariah (9:9) may be in Mark's thoughts as he describes the preparations for the entry of Jesus into Jerusalem, not on a horse but humbly on a donkey. Jesus tells his disciples to bring a young donkey from a village.

It may have been a previous arrangement with the owner, or the meaning may be that it is God who wants the donkey for his Messiah and shall bring it back with his Messiah sitting upon it.

Some of the disciples spontaneously place their garments on the donkey. Others spread them on the roadway before him, which again reminds us of the 'way' along which Jesus leads his disciples. Others cut leafy branches from the fields on the Mount of Olives.

Some disciples go before him and some follow, but without the great crowds which we find in the Gospel of Matthew. They joyfully sing 'Hosanna', which literally means 'Please save' and was commonly used as a joyful cry of praise to God. They shout and sing together that Jesus is the one blessed by God who is coming to Jerusalem in his name.

He comes as a humble servant ready to give even his life, to ransom the people into the freedom of God's kingdom. His humble entry reveals he is the Messiah to those who have faith in God, but conceals it from those who seek a different kind of Messiah.

Jesus enters the temple. He looks around and then with the twelve leaves the city to spend the night at Bethany on the Mount of Olives. Does he not feel safe?

12 On the following day, when they came from Bethany, he was hungry. 13 Seeing in the distance a fig tree in leaf, he went to see whether perhaps he would find anything on it. When he came to it, he found nothing but leaves, for it was not the season for figs. 14 He said to it, 'May no one ever eat fruit from you again.' And his disciples heard it.

15 Then they came to Jerusalem. And he entered the temple and began to drive out those who were selling and those who were buying in the temple, and he overturned the tables of the money changers and the seats of those who sold doves; 16 and he would not allow anyone to carry anything through the temple. 17 He was teaching and saying, 'Is it not written, "My house shall be called a house of prayer for all the nations"? But you have made it a den of robbers.' 18 And when the chief priests and the scribes heard it, they kept looking for a way to kill him; for they were afraid of him, because the whole crowd was spellbound by his teaching. 19 And when evening came, Jesus and his disciples went out of the city.

20 In the morning as they passed, they saw the fig tree withered away to its roots. 21 Then Peter remembered and said to him, 'Rabbi, look! The fig tree that you cursed has withered.' 22 Jesus answered them, 'Have faith in God. 23 Truly I tell you, if you say to this mountain, "Be taken up and thrown into the sea," and if you do not doubt in your heart, but believe that what you say will come to pass, it will be done for you. 24 So I tell you, whatever you ask for in prayer, believe that you have received it, and it will be yours. 25 Whenever you stand praying, forgive, if you have anything against anyone; so that your Father who is in heaven may also forgive you your trespasses.'

Starters

1. Why do you feel the people and the priests react so differently to the same teaching of Jesus in the temple?
2. Consider why the teaching of Jesus on prayer is linked so closely with his teaching on forgiveness of others.

VI/2. Jesus purifies the temple

The dramatic cleansing of the temple in Jerusalem is another example where Mark sandwiches one event between the two halves of another. The story of the fig tree frames, before and after, the story of the temple cleansing. By this Mark says one story helps to understand the other.

The next day, as Jesus with the twelve leaves Bethany to enter Jerusalem for the second time, they find a fig tree with leaves but no fruit. This episode may have first been a parable of Jesus which in a community tradition over the years, before Mark wrote, became an actual happening, to give more point to the teaching. The cursing of a tree for having no fruit at the wrong season is unlike the usual behaviour of Jesus.

Jesus sees the temple as a place of sterile worship and rejects it. It does not give a true witness to God's power coming into the world. In a symbolic action, characteristic of the great prophets of the Old Testament, Jesus takes back the temple from those who have 'stolen' it for national interests and secular concerns, to make it a place for all peoples.

He begins to teach there, making it a house of prayer for all. The people listen to his words, but the priests and scribes look for ways to destroy him. When evening comes he leaves Jerusalem.

Next morning they enter the city for the third time and find the fig tree withered. It is a symbol of the eventual destruction of the temple, where other things have replaced true faith in God. It also symbolises persons lacking faith that bears fruit.

True prayer rises from responsiveness to God in faith and always bears fruit, even fruits humanly impossible. Prayer in true faith, Jesus teaches, is always open to forgive others. Only then can God's action effectively reach those who pray.

Mark 11:27-33

27 *Again they came to Jerusalem. As he was walking in the temple, the chief priests, the scribes, and the elders came to him* 28 *and said, 'By what authority are you doing these things? Who gave you this authority to do them?'*

29 *Jesus said to them, 'I will ask you one question; answer me, and I will tell you by what authority I do these things.*

30 *Did the baptism of John come from heaven, or was it of human origin? Answer me.'*

31 *They argued with one another, 'If we say, "From heaven," he will say, "Why then did you not believe him?"*

32 *'But shall we say, "Of human origin"?'* — *they were afraid of the crowd for all regarded John as truly a real prophet.*

33 *So they answered Jesus, 'We do not know.' And Jesus said to them, 'Neither will I tell you by what authority I am doing these things.'*

Starters

1. *Imagine a similar hostile questioning of Jesus by powerful political, commercial, learned or religious leaders today.*

2. *Imagine yourself meeting Jesus in the temple after this event. What might be say to you?*

3. *When I pray, do I ever let God question the origins of the things I bring to him in prayer, my motives or my sincerity?*

VI/3. Jesus meets the Jerusalem leaders

For the fourth time, Jesus enters Jerusalem and the temple. As he walks in the open courts of the temple, some of the city leaders come to him and confront him in a hostile manner.

In the group are priests, scribes and elders, who represent the religious, learned and political elite of Jerusalem as well as powerful commercial and business interests. They want to know from Jesus by what authority he stopped the buying and selling of things needed for sacrifice and worship. The implication is that Jesus needs authority from God for such actions.

Jesus will answer them only if they first answer his question. It was an established practice among Jewish rabbis to answer one question with another, so what Jesus does is not unusual. The question of Jesus about the baptism of John makes these leaders look into the motives and sincerity of their question to him. It forces them to look at their own lack of faith in God, which is at the roots of their hostility towards his actions in the temple.

Since John proclaimed himself the humble forerunner preparing the way for the Messiah, the question of Jesus about him implies also the question of his own identity as the Messiah from God. To answer the question of Jesus in either way will reveal their duplicity and their lack of genuine faith in God. Apparently it was common knowledge that they themselves had not accepted John the baptiser as a real prophet, which the people did.

When the leaders refuse to answer him, Jesus will not answer their question about the source of his own authority. Like all the others who see what Jesus does and hear what he teaches, they must decide for themselves who he is. Is Jesus truly from God with God's authority? Is he really sent to reveal God's power in the world?

Mark 12:1-12

1 Then he began to speak to them in parables. 'A man planted a vineyard, put a fence around it, and dug a pit for the wine press, and built a watch-tower; then he leased it to tenants and went to another country.

2 'When the season came, he sent a slave to the tenants to collect from them his share of the produce of the vineyard. 3 But they seized him, and beat him, and sent him away empty-handed. 4 And again he sent another slave to them, this one they beat over the head and insulted. 5 Then he sent another, and that one they killed. And so with many others; some they beat, and others they killed.

6 'He had still one other, a beloved son. Finally he sent him to them, saying, "They will respect my son."

7 'But those tenants said to one another, "This is the heir; come, let us kill him, and the inheritance will be ours."

8 'So they seized him, killed him, and threw him out of the vineyard.

9 'What then will the owner of the vineyard do? He will come and destroy the tenants and give the vineyard to others.

10 Have you not read this scripture: "The very stone which the builders rejected has become the head of the corner; 11 this was the Lord's doing, and it is amazing in our eyes"?'

12 When they realised that he had told this parable against them, they wanted to arrest him, but they feared the crowd. So they left him and went away.

Starters

1. *Search for a situation in your life today where the parable of Jesus about the vineyard might have a meaning for you.*

2. *Pray for persons called to be God's servants and messengers in places and situations where they are treated badly.*

VI /4. The parable of the vineyard

Mark has placed this parable of Jesus after the confrontation with Jesus by the Jerusalem leaders in the temple. Their hostility already points to their final rejection of him and their condemnation of him to death.

The parable of Jesus about a vineyard is not directed to his disciples, as his earlier parables were, but to his opponents, the Jewish leaders who confronted him and challenged his authority. It is a parable of God seeking the fruits of true faith from a people whom he has repeatedly nourished through many prophets and holy people, and now through his beloved son, the Son of God (1:11, 9:7).

The parable has obvious allegorical implications in its different details, and Jesus himself seems to have intended these. The Jews who first hear the parable, as well as the early Christians at the time when Mark wrote, would see these allegorical details. The vineyard carefully planted and lovingly cared for by God, is a common metaphor for the people of Israel in the writings of the Old Testament (Ps 80:8, Is 5:1, Jer 2:21). The tenant farmers who cultivate the vineyard during the owner's absence are the leaders of Israel, the priests, the scribes and the elders of the people. The slaves who are sent by the owner of the vineyard and badly treated by the farmers are the persecuted prophets of the Old Testament. The son killed by the farmers is Jesus as the Messiah, rejected and crucified by the Jerusalem authorities.

The teaching of Jesus about the corner-stone which holds the whole building together quotes a psalm in the Old Testament (118:22-23). It implies a final vindication of Jesus by God.

The Jerusalem leaders do not listen, but see only an attack upon themselves as leaders in Israel. The last sentence underlines their wilful separation from Jesus and their continuing hostility to him.

13 Then they sent to him some Pharisees and some Herodians to trap him in what he said.

14 And they came and said to him, 'Teacher, we know that you are sincere, and show deference to no one; for you do not regard people with partiality, but teach the way of God in accordance with truth. Is it lawful to pay taxes to the emperor, or not?

15 'Should we pay them, or should we not?' But knowing their hypocrisy, he said to them, 'Why are you putting me to the test? Bring me a denarius and let me see it.'

16 And they brought one. Then he said to them, 'Whose hand is this and whose title?' They said to him, 'The emperor's.'

17 Jesus said to them, 'Give to the emperor the things that are the emperor's, and to God the things that are God's.' And they were utterly amazed at him.

Starters

1. *Ponder the description of Jesus given here, apparently current among the people at the time, as a teacher of the way of God.*

2. *God has put his image upon each one. How ready am I to entrust myself totally to God?*

VI/5. The image on a coin

The priests, scribes and elders failed in their attack on Jesus (11:27-33), so they send some Pharisees and some Herodians to trap him and discredit him before the people. The Pharisees were zealous for the strict observance of the law of Moses that was adapted to their own times. The Herodians were political nationalists, supporters of Herod Antipas. Both groups seemed to show tolerance towards the presence in Israel of the Roman occupying power. Neither was actively rebellious against Roman occupation as the zealots were.

Their flattery of Jesus, as one who teaches faithfully 'the way of God', may reflect the popular estimation of him, at least among those coming from Galilee.

The question about taxes is an attempt to upset Jesus. If he answers yes, the people of Jerusalem will reject him as a collaborator with the Romans. If he answers no, the Roman authorities in Jerusalem will take action against him. As before with the Jerusalem leaders, he answers by putting his own question, asking whose image is on the money they use in Jerusalem.

On a silver Roman denarius at the time was the image of the Roman Emperor Tiberius (4-37 AD) and the words, 'Tiberius Caesar, son of the divine Augustus, the high priest.' These were blasphemous words for a Jew. Nevertheless, the Jews used Roman coins, thereby admitting Roman authority, even though they changed the foreign money into Jewish coins for their temple offerings.

Without directly answering their question, Jesus makes his teaching clear. Since the image of Caesar is on the coin, then in some way it belongs to him, so give it back to him. The just demands of secular authority are to be respected. Since men and women are made in the image of God, as every Jew believed, then each one belongs to God and is called to give oneself back to God!

18 *Some Sadducees, who say there is no resurection, came to him and asked him a question, saying,* 19 *'Teacher, Moses wrote for us that "if a man's brother dies, leaving a wife but no child, the man shall marry the widow and raise up children for his brother."*

20 *'There were seven brothers; the first married and, when he died, left no children;* 21 *and the second married her and died, leaving no children; and the third likewise;* 22 *none of the seven left children. Last of all the woman herself died.* 23 *In the resurrection whose wife will she be? For the seven had married her.'*

24 *Jesus said to them, 'Is not this the reason you are wrong, that you know neither the scriptures nor the power of God?*

25 *'For when they rise from the dead, they neither marry nor are given in marriage, but are like angels in heaven.*

26 *'And as for the dead being raised, have you not read in the book of Moses, in the story about the bush, how God said to him, "I am the God of Abraham, the God of Isaac, and the God of Jacob"?*

27 *'He is God not of the dead, but of the living; you are quite wrong.'*

Starters

1. *Let me look at Jesus after the Sadducees left and try to feel within myself Jesus' own faith in God's power to raise.*

2. *Ponder the love I feel for those close to me, and feel with Jesus how great this love will become in our risen lives.*

VI/6. The resurrection

A third time, Jesus is presented with a question from his enemies, this time from the Sadducees, the only occasion they are mentioned in Mark's Gospel. Sadducees were the hereditary priestly caste, more political than religious in their interests, who were from the leading families of the Jerusalem establishment. From them the high priest was chosen. They were conservative, in contrast to the progressive Pharisees, and based themselves chiefly on the five books of the law, the Pentateuch or first part of the Old Testament. They questioned belief in angels and spirits and in personal immortality after death.

Like the Pharisees and Herodians, they come to discredit Jesus in the eyes of the people. They propose a situation which they think makes resurrection after death impossible. Their question presumes a Jewish custom concerning the obligation of a dead man's brother or nearest relative. The answer of Jesus, as Mark tells it, has two main truths. One is the manner of resurrection, the other the fact of resurrection.

There will be no marrying, Jesus says, in the risen life, but all will be like angels in heaven. Angels in Jewish understanding at the time were not primarily beings without bodies, but beings who lived always in God's presence and who served God by bringing to men and women a universal concern for all things. Jesus is not saying that husbands and wives will love each other less intimately in the life after death, but that they will love others more, without the exclusiveness which is in married love now.

Secondly, Jesus bluntly tells the Sadducees they are wrong to deny the resurrection. In the law, which they accept, Moses on the mountain saw God as the God of Abraham, of Isaac and of Jacob. All of these were long dead at the time of Moses. A relation with an eternal God stretches beyond death.

Mark 12:28-34

28 One of the scribes came near and heard them disputing with one another, and seeing that he answered them well, he asked him, 'Which commandment is the first of all?'

29 Jesus answered, 'The first is, "Hear, O Israel: the Lord our God, the Lord is one; 30 you shall love the Lord your God with all your heart, and with all your soul, and with all your mind, and with all your strength."

31 'The second is this, "You shall love your neighbour as yourself." There is no other commandment greater than these.'

32 Then the scribe said to him, 'You are right, Teacher: you have truly said that "he is one, and besides him there is no other; 33 and "to love him with all the heart, and with all the understanding, and with all the strength", and "to love one's neighbour as oneself" — this is much more important than all whole burnt offerings and sacrifices.'

34 When Jesus saw that he answered wisely, he said to him, 'You are not far from the kingdom of God.' And after that no one dared to ask him any question.

Starters

1. Read the passage again to get a better feel of the friendly relation between Jesus and the Scribe.

2. Dwell a little on the big difference between doing something because you are commanded and doing it because you want to.

VI/7. Jesus and a friendly scribe

The previous questions to Jesus in the temple at Jerusalem have been asked in a hostile manner, first from the Jerusalem leaders about authority (11:27-33), then from the Pharisees and Herodians about taxes (12:13-17), and thirdly from the Sadducees about resurrection (12:18-27). A fourth question, in Mark's Gospel at least, is not hostile, but comes from a friendly scribe.

He puts a question to Jesus for which he and all those who studied the law of Moses with care had yet to find a convincing answer. Which is the commandment that is the first of all in God's law, the one which grounds all the others?

The answer of Jesus surprises the scribe, for Jesus does not give one commandment but two, which he links together as one. He teaches that love for God cannot be apart from love for one another. He answers by two quotations from the Old Testament. One is taken from the Book of Deuteronomy (6:4). This is the *shema* prayer, said by all devout Jews each morning and evening. The other is from the Book of Leviticus (19:18) which most Jews, it appears, applied to fellow Jews only.

The choice of these two texts, and especially linking them as one, delights the friendly scribe. How much greater, he exclaims enthusiastically, is this kind of love than even the most solemn sacrifices of the temple!

Jesus tells him that he is coming close to the kingdom of God. Yet he is not yet within that kingdom. He has still to experience something greater than keeping commandments, even greater than the first command of all, which is to love God and the second to love one's neighbour. This something is God's gift of divine life and love to us, the central experience of the kingdom of God and the heart of the gospel Jesus proclaims. No more questions come to Jesus after that.

35 While Jesus was teaching in the temple, he said, 'How can the scribes say that the Messiah is the son of David?

36 'David himself, by the Holy Spirit, declared, ''The Lord said to my Lord, Sit at my right hand, until I put your enemies under your feet.''

37 'David himself calls him Lord; so how can he be his son?' And the large crowd heard him with delight.

38 As he taught, he said, 'Beware of the scribes, who like to walk about in long robes, and to be greeted with respect in the marketplace, 39 and to have the best seats in the synagogues and the places of honour at banquets!

40 'They devour widows' houses and for the sake of appearances say long prayers. They will receive the greater condemnation.'

Starters

1. How do I imagine Jesus feels in himself as he speaks of these scribes in this way?

2. Speak to Jesus about his attitude towards poor widows and others like them today who have to struggle through life alone.

VI/8. A question of Jesus for the people

The fifth question in this part of Mark's Gospel (11:27—12:40) comes from Jesus himself. He puts the question apparently to all who are listening to him in the temple at Jerusalem. It is about the identity of the expected Messiah as the Son of David, which the scribes taught he will be. It raises in the hearts of his listeners the mystery of his own identity.

The popular expectation of the Jews was for a Messiah descended from King David, who lived around 1000 BC. He was generally accepted at the time of Jesus to be the author of the psalm which Jesus quotes (Ps 110:1), though it was likely written much later, even only two hundred years before Christ.

Jesus does not doubt the Messiah will be a descendant of David. What he asks the people is how can the scribes explain the opening words of this psalm, the Lord (God) says to my Lord (the Messiah). How can David call my Lord one of his own descendants, Jesus asks, unless that descendant is someone more than just his descendant?

The common people are delighted with the teaching of Jesus, but many of the scribes, whose role was to study the Scriptures and to interpret them for the common people, are surely not. They refuse to see in Jesus, someone who could be greater than David, their soldier-king.

The harsh words of Jesus, which follow (38-40) against the pride, hyprocrisy and greed of the learned scribes must have some basis in his actual life, but they probably also echo something of the hostile situation of confrontation between early Christian communities and first century Judaism at the time when Mark wrote. Jesus observes things that point to the arrogance, the vanity, the greed and the hyprocrisy of the scribes. They are resisting the power of God and bringing condemnation on themselves.

Mark 12:41-44

41 He sat down opposite the treasury, and watched the crowd putting money into the treasury. Many rich people put in large sums.

42 A poor widow came and put in two small copper coins, which are worth a penny.

43 Then he called his disciples and said to them, 'Truly I tell you, this poor widow has put in more than all those who are contributing to the treasury.

44 'For all of them have contributed out of their abundance; but she out of her poverty has put in everything she had, all she had to live on.'

Starters

1. *Look at Jesus sitting in the temple court and speak with him about the widow he is watching.*

2. *Is the total giving of oneself to God practical for human living today? Talk with Jesus now risen as the Christ, about this.*

VI/9. The widow's offering

The section of Mark's Gospel (11:1 — 12:44), which describes the teaching of Jesus in the temple at Jerusalem, concludes with the brief story of a poor widow. What adds to its human appeal is the scene of Jesus sitting silently in one of the temple courts, observing how the different people come to throw their money into one of the trumpet-shaped chests placed along the walls to receive the offerings.

The widow is poor, one of the common people who welcome Jesus with delight (12:37). The contrast between her humble gesture and the behaviour of the scribes in the previous story is stark. Their actions were seen by Jesus to be proud and hypocritical. The widow's action is sincere, and her offering to God is total.

The two little copper coins may have been 'lepta', the smallest coins in circulation at Jerusalem. Two of them would add to no more than one cent. Her gift in itself is practically valueless.

Jesus emphasises the importance of what he says by the characteristic expression, 'truly (amen) I say to you'. How Jesus comes to know all about the widow does not interest Mark.

He does not necessarily suggest that the knowledge of Jesus is supernatural. He surprises his disciples by saying that the poor widow has given more than all the others. Jesus holds up her action as a model of the total giving of oneself to God which he asks of his disciples.

This is the last of all the teachings of Jesus in the temple at Jerusalem. Mark places it here as a kind of climax to all that Jesus has taught in the temple, in fact, to all his teaching for the disciples about his 'way', since the time at Caesarea Philippi (8:31). It sums up his teaching on the need in true disciples for total surrender. The widow offers all she has to God.

Mark 13:1-4

1 As he came out of the temple, one of his disciples said to him, 'Look, Teacher, what large stones and what large buildings!'

2 Then Jesus asked him, 'Do you see these great buildings? Not one stone will be left here upon another; all will be thrown down.'

3 When he was sitting on the Mount of Olives opposite the temple, Peter, James, John and Andrew asked him privately,

4 'Tell us, when will this be, and what will be the sign that all these things are about to be accomplished?'

Starters

1. Try to share the feelings of Jesus as he spoke to his disciples of the coming destruction of the Jerusalem temple and of all that it symbolised for Israel.

2. Picture for yourself Jesus sitting on the slope of the Mount of Olives and looking across the valley towards Jerusalem and the temple on the other side.

3. Notice how the two questions asked by three of his first disciples prepare us for what Jesus will say to them about his hope for the future.

VI/10. Jesus leaves the temple

After his brief ministry in Jerusalem where he taught the people in the temple each day, but at night returned to Bethany and did not remain in the city (chapters 11-12), Jesus leaves the temple for the last time.

His time in Jerusalem has been marked by opposition from the leading people. It will not be long before this economic, political, cultural, intellectual and religious centre of Israel will finally reject him altogether and have him put to death.

Two little scenes introduce chapter 13 and both are focused on the temple.

As Jesus is leaving the temple for the last time, one of his disciples is full of admiration for the greatness of the temple buildings, but Jesus says it will all soon be gone (1-2). Faith in God must be expressed in more than stones and mortar.

Later, after Jesus has left the city, he sits with his disciples on the slopes of the Mount of Olives which overlooks the temple from the east. Privately, three of his first disciples ask him two questions, when the destruction will come, and what will be its sign (3-4)?

These two questions from the inner circle of Jesus' disciples introduce the rest of chapter 13. This chapter gives the teaching of Jesus about the future in the form of a little 'apocalypse', a popular way among the Jews at the time of Jesus for presenting religious teaching.

5 *Jesus began to say to them, 'Beware that no one leads you astray.* 6 *Many will come in my name and say, "I am he!" and they will lead many astray.* 7 *When you hear of wars and rumors of wars, do not be alarmed; this must take place, but the end is still to come.* 8 *For nation will rise against nation, and kingdom against kingdom; there will be earthquakes in various places; there will be famines. This is but the beginning of the birth-pangs.* 9 *'As for yourselves, beware; for they will hand you over to councils; and you will be beaten in synagogues; and you will stand before governors and kings because of me, as a testimony to them.* 10 *And the good news must first be proclaimed to all nations.* 11 *When they bring you to trial and hand you over, do not worry beforehand about what you are to say; but say whatever is given you at that time, for it is not you who speak, but the Holy Spirit.* 12 *Brother will betray brother to death, and a father his child, and children will rise against parents and have them put to death;* 13 *and you will be hated by all because of my name. But the one who endures to the end will be saved.*

14 *'But when you see the desolating sacrilege set up where it ought not to be (let the reader understand), then those in Judea must flee to the mountains;* 15 *the one on the housetop must not go down or enter the house to take anything away;* 16 *the one in the field must not turn back to get a coat.* 17 *Woe to those who are pregnant and to those who are nursing infants in those days!* 18 *Pray that it may not be in the winter.* 19 *For in those days there will be suffering, such as has not been from the beginning of the creation that God created until now, no, and never will be.* 20 *And if the Lord had not cut short those days, no one would be saved; but for the sake of the elect, whom he chose, he has cut short those days.* 21 *And if anyone says to you at that time, "Look! Here is the Messiah!" or "Look! There he is!" — do not believe it.* 22 *False messiahs and false prophets will appear and produce signs and omens, to lead astray, if possible, the elect.* 23 *But be alert, I have already told you everything.*

VI/11. Jesus shares his future hope

Jesus does not directly answer the two questions which his three disciples have put to him (13:3-4), but he describes in apocalyptic style a terrible desecration of the temple, something the Romans actually did in the year 70, during the Roman-Jewish war (66-74).

An 'apocalypse' is a literary way of presenting God's saving action, already coming into the world in the present, by creating imaginative descriptions of its final victory over evil in future destructive events and cosmic upheavals in the world.

It is likely that here Mark has elaborated the work of an earlier Christian author, who to give encouragement and hope to fellow Christians composed a little apocalypse incorporating teachings of Jesus about the future.

This short apocalypse, by which Mark ends his narrative of the ministry of Jesus in Jerusalem, has two parts. There are the signs surrounding the destruction of Jerusalem (13:5-23), and the signs accompanying the coming of the Messiah (13:24-37).

In these teachings Jesus invites his disciples to enter into his hope for the future. Around a central teaching (14), Mark appears to have arranged the other teachings of Jesus in three parts of successive 'frames', or pairs of teachings. Awareness of this literary structure helps to a better understanding.

True disciples must be alert and not be deceived by false prophets (5-6 and 21-23). They must not despair when they see wars and natural calamities (7-8 and 19-20).

When persecutions and betrayals come, they must not become anxious but remain watchful for God's powerful action, even when they have to flee from Jerusalem (9-13 and 15-18).

24 'But in those days, after that suffering, the sun will be darkened, and the moon will not give its light, 25 and the stars will be falling from heaven, and the powers in the heavens will be shaken. 26 Then they will see "the Son of Man coming in clouds" with great power and glory. 27 Then he will send out the angels, and gather his elect from the four winds, from the ends of the earth to the ends of heaven.

28 'From the fig tree learn its lesson: as soon as its branch becomes tender and puts forth its leaves, you know that summer is near. 29 So also, when you see these things taking place, you know that he is near, at the very gates. 30 Truly I tell you, this generation will not pass away until all these things have taken place. 31 Heaven and earth will pass away, but my words will not pass away.

32 'But about that day or hour no one knows, neither the angels in heaven, nor the Son, but only the Father. 33 Beware, keep alert; for you do not know when the time will come.

34 'It is like a man going on a journey, when he leaves home and puts his slaves in charge, each with his work, and commands the doorkeeper to be on the watch. 35 Therefore, keep awake — for you do not know when the master of the house will come, in the evening, or at midnight, or at cockcrow, or at dawn, 36 or else he may find you asleep when he comes suddenly.

37 And what I say to you I say to all: Keep awake.'

Starters

1. Look at Jesus as he sits with his disciples on the mountain and speaks of Jerusalem and the temple and times of testing. Can I feel his hope?

2. Reflect how faith is presented here as 'watchfulness'.

3. Look back at the whole ministry of Jesus which has brought him from the lake in Galilee to the mountain at Jerusalem.

VI/12. The last teaching of Jesus

The second portion of the teaching of Jesus about the future has a different focus. It is the future coming of God's Messiah in glory (24-27). His coming will be accompanied by cosmic upheavals and changes in the world (25). He will come as the leader who unifies the world (26), and he will gather together those faithful to God from all regions of the world (27).

The Son of Man coming in the glory and power of God is a reference to the prophecy of Daniel (7:13-14), but also points to the enigmatic name Jesus uses for himself in Mark's Gospel.

When Mark wrote, probably in the early seventies, he and other Christians may have expected the coming of the Messiah in glory in their own time. That was not to be, as we know two thousand years later. Yet by his resurrection Jesus has come already as the Messiah. He is with us in a partially hidden way which reveals his presence among us by different signs, while we await his final coming in future glory.

Jesus teaches that not even he knows the time of that future coming. The secret of the Father alone is put by Mark at the centre of these teachings (32). Preceding it, we find the little parable of the fig-tree (28-29), the teaching on the nearness of the Messiah's return (30), and the certainty of the future hope of Jesus (31). Following that central teaching, watchfulness is mentioned in almost every verse.

The disciples must be on the watch always (33). The need to watch for the Messiah is taught in a short parable about a man who went away on a journey (34-36). The sum of all Jesus wants to say to his disciples about the future is to be watchful (37).

Mark's apocalypse helps us feel the sure hope of Jesus for the future and the urgency of his last teaching, 'Keep awake'!

─────── VII ───────

JESUS DIES ON A CROSS

Mark 14:1 — 16:8

Mark 14:1-11

1 It was two days before the Passover and the festival of Unleavened Bread. The chief priests and the scribes were looking for a way to arrest him by stealth and kill him; 2 for they said, 'Not during the festival, or there may be a riot among the people.'

3 While he was at Bethany in the house of Simon the leper, as he sat at table, a woman came with an alabaster jar of very costly ointment of nard, and she broke open the jar and poured the ointment on his head.

4 But some were there who said to one another in anger, 'Why was the ointment wasted in this way? 5 For this ointment could have been sold for more than three hundred denarii, and the money given to the poor.' And they scolded her.

6 But Jesus said, 'Let her alone; why do you trouble her? She has done a good service for me.

7 'For you always have the poor with you, and you can show kindness to them whenever you wish; but you will not always have me.

8 She has done what she could; she has anointed my body beforehand for its burial.

9 Truly I tell you, wherever the good news is proclaimed in the whole world, what she has done will be told in remembrance of her.'

10 Then Judas Iscariot, who was one of the twelve, went to the chief priests in order to betray him to them.

11 When they heard it, they were greatly pleased, and promised to give him money. So he began to look for an opportunity to betray him.

Starters

1. *Ponder a little the devotion and fidelity of this woman at Bethany.*
2. *Contrast the act of the woman with the grumbling of the others.*

VII/1. The anointing at Bethany

The story of the suffering and death of Jesus begins with his anointing. It is done during a meal at Bethany by an unnamed woman. Bethany was a village close to Jerusalem, at the top of the Mount of Olives on its eastern side.

The act of a woman at the beginning of the story of the passion of Jesus parallels the devotion of the women at its end. After watching his death and burial, women come to anoint the body of Jesus (16:1-8). The faithfulness of women 'frames' the unfaithfulness of men in the passion story.

In the woman's gesture, Jesus is symbolically proclaimed as the anointed one, or the Messiah, of God. With thoughts of his approaching death before him, Jesus points to a further depth of meaning in what the woman has done. Neither she nor the others could have understood the full significance of her action as an anointing for his burial.

Jesus strongly affirms that her act will later be remembered wherever the gospel of his death and resurrection is proclaimed by his disciples (9).

The story of the woman's act of faithfulness is framed between the plot of the priests and scribes to kill Jesus (14:1-2) and the unfaithfulness of Judas, one of the twelve (14:10-11).

The lack of understanding in those present, apparently disciples and friends, is mentioned. Some grumble at what they consider to be a waste of money. The cost of such a jar of ointment, at three hundred denarii, was about one year's wages of an ordinary worker.

Many think the whole passion narrative was the first part of the story of Jesus to be told or written down in the first Christian communities, so that the events of chapters 14-16 may have existed as some kind of continuous story before Mark creatively incorporated it into his Gospel.

Mark 14:12-25

12 On the first day of Unleavened Bread, when the Passover lamb is sacrificed, his disciples said to him, 'Where do you want us go and make the preparations for you to eat the Passover?'

13 So he sent two of his disciples, saying to them, 'Go into the city, and a man carrying a jar of water will meet you; follow him, 14 and wherever he enters, say to the owner of the house, "The Teacher asks, Where is my guest room, where I may eat the Passover with my disciples?" 15 He will show you a large room upstairs, furnished and ready. Make preparations for us there.'

16 So the disciples set out and went to the city, and found everything as he had told them; and they prepared the Passover meal.

17 When it was evening, he came with the twelve.

18 And when they had taken their places and were eating, Jesus said, 'Truly I tell you, one of you will betray me, one who is eating with me.' 19 They began to be distressed and to say to him one after another, 'Surely, not I?' 20 He said to them, 'It is one of the twelve, one who is dipping bread into the bowl with me. 21 For the Son of Man goes as it is written of him, but woe to that one by whom the Son of Man is betrayed! It would have been better for that one not to have been born.'

22 While they were eating, he took a loaf of bread, and after blessing it he broke it, and gave it to them, and said, 'Take; this is my body.' 23 Then he took a cup, and after giving thanks he gave it to them, and all of them drank from it. 24 He said to them, 'This is my blood of the covenant, which is poured out for many. 25 Truly I tell you, I will never again drink of the fruit of the vine until that day when I drink it new in the kingdom of God.'

Starters

1. Imagine the setting and feel the atmosphere of this last meal of Jesus.
2. Ponder the interior attitude of Jesus towards God and his disciples as he shared himself with them through the bread and wine.

VII/2. The last meal with his disciples

Mark presents the last meal of Jesus with his disciples as a passover meal of thanksgiving, and tells the story of its preparation in a way similar to the preparation for the entry into Jerusalem (11:1-6). Mark says nothing explicitly of the killing of a lamb and the other things needed for a passover meal.

In the evening when they take their places around the table, Jesus announces in strong language, 'truly (amen), I say to you', that one of the twelve eating with him will betray him.

This last meal of Jesus with his disciples is 'framed', before and after, by their infidelity. He speaks first of his betrayal by one of them (18), and later of the public denial of him by another (30). Jesus is not threatening his disciples, but emphasising the unfaithfulness among his close followers who gather to eat with him at the same table.

The last meal of Jesus reaches its climax in the ritual actions of Jesus with bread and wine taken from the table. These gestures of Jesus and his accompanying words have been recognised from the earliest years of Christian faith as the institution of the Christian eucharist or thanksgiving meal.

Jesus took some bread from the table, said a prayer of praise to God over the bread, and then broke it for his disciples to eat. He told them that this eating together was the visible embodiment of his own person in the world. Then he did the same with a cup of wine, which he called his own blood of the covenant (Ex 24:8) to be poured out by him for all.

At the end of the meal, Jesus emphatically assures the twelve that he will eat with them again in a new manner, when the kingdom of God has come, that is, when God shows the fulness of his power in glory.

26 *When they had sung the hymn, they went out to the Mount of Olives.*

27 *And Jesus said to them, 'You will all become deserters; for it is written, "I will strike the shepherd, and the sheep will be scattered."*

28 *'But after I am raised up, I will go before you to Galilee.'*

29 *Peter said to him, 'Even though they all become deserters, I will not.'*

30 *Jesus said to him, 'Truly I tell you, this very night, before the cock crows twice, you will deny me three times.'*

31 *But he said vehemently, 'Even though I must die with you, I will not deny you.' And all of them said the same.*

Starters

1. Contrast Judas going off to betray Jesus with the other disciples, till now still faithful and going with him to Gethsemane.

2. Consider how in spite of the infidelity of his disciples Jesus promises that he will be with them again in Galilee.

VII/3. The unfaithfulness of the disciples

At the end of the meal, Jesus and his disciples sing a hymn of praise, and then depart together for the Mount of Olives. They leave the upstairs room, probably in the south-western part of the city, and may have walked outside the city walls to a small countryplace nearby called Gethsemani on the lower part of the slope of the Mount of Olives, outside the eastern wall of the city. Judas appears to have already left the group and gone to betray Jesus.

As they walk to Gethsemane, Jesus speaks of a desertion by all his disciples, and a public denial by one of them, Peter. Plots and infidelity formed the setting before and after the meal at Bethany. Now, before and after the last meal in Jerusalem, Jesus speaks of unfaithfulness.

The words of the prophet Zechariah (Zech 13:7-9), who lived in the fifth century BC after the time of the exile of the Jews in Babylon, give the setting. When the shepherd is struck down the sheep will be scattered, but after this time of testing they will all be gathered together once more as God's people.

Again Jesus briefly refers to his future vindication by God in resurrection (28). He has done this already several times, on the mountain and in the three prophecies of his passion (9:9 and 8:31, 9:31, 10:34).

Then Jesus tells his disciples that after he is raised, he will go before them all into Galilee. Galilee is the place of beginnings for the disciples, where Jesus first called them to be disciples, and where they followed him and witnessed his first proclamations of the gospel. The mention of Galilee hints of new beginnings for the disciples after Jesus has been raised by God.

The disciples reply confidently that they will never become deserters. Their rash confidence challenges us to look with honesty at our faithfulness.

32 They went to a place called Gethsemane; and he said to his disciples, 'Sit here, while I pray.'

33 He took with him Peter and James and John, and began to be distressed and agitated.

34 And he said to them, 'I am deeply grieved, even to death; remain here, and keep awake.'

35 And going a little farther, he threw himself on the ground and prayed that, if it were possible, the hour might pass from him.

36 He said, 'Abba, Father, for you all things are possible; remove this cup from me; yet, not what I want, but what you want.'

37 He came and found them sleeping, and he said to Peter, 'Simon, are you asleep? Could you not keep awake one hour?

38 'Keep awake and pray that you may not come into the time of trial; the spirit indeed is willing, but the flesh is weak.'

39 And again he went away and prayed, saying the same words.

40 And once more he came and found them sleeping, for their eyes were very heavy; and they did not know what to say to him.

41 He came the third time, and said to them, 'Are you still sleeping and taking your rest? Enough! The hour has come; the Son of Man is betrayed into the hands of sinners.

42 Get up, let us be going. See, my betrayer is at hand.'

Starter

Notice the three strong verbs Mark uses in verses 33 and 34 to express the interior state of Jesus as he goes to pray.

VII/4. The prayer in Gethsemane

Jesus and his disciples arrive at Gethsemane, which means an oil-press and suggests a farm planted with olive trees. He takes with him Peter, James and John, the three who were with him on the mountain when he was named his Son by God (9:2).

Before he prays, Jesus is seized by a terrible fear. The words used by Mark express the strongest and deepest human feelings. Jesus loses his usual calm and strength and becomes restless, troubled and confused. He cries out to the three disciples accompanying him that he is drowning in a sorrow like death. He appears weak and seems to look to his disciples for human support.

Yet it is clear that it is Jesus in his weakness and confusion who is really the strong one and that the three disciples in their inability to watch are the ones in need of help.

'Abba', my own father, papa, or some similar intimate name, which sons and daughters would use of a father within the family, is the word Jesus uses. He prays that he may be spared the cup of suffering and condemnation.

Jesus may have once hoped for success but now he sees his mission as doomed to human failure. Yet the centre of his prayer remains his mission from God, what God wills, not his own weakness and fears. His inner spirit is willing but his human flesh, like his disciples', is weak. The commitment of Jesus to his mission contrasts starkly with the weakness of his human fears.

The approach of Judas, the one who will hand him over, is the visible sign that the hour of testing has come. He summons his disciples to face with him this testing.

The prayer of Jesus in Gethsemane invites us to share the experience in Jesus himself of faithful service in interior suffering and pain.

Mark 14:43-52

43 *Immediately, while he was still speaking, Judas, one of the twelve, arrived and with him there was a crowd with swords and clubs, from the chief priests, the scribes and the elders.*

44 *Now the betrayer had given them a sign, saying, 'The one I will kiss is the man; arrest him and lead him away underguard.'*

45 *So when he came, he went up to him at once and said, 'Rabbi!' and kissed him.*

46 *Then they laid hands on him and arrested him.*

47 *But one of those who stood near drew his sword, and struck the slave of the high priest, cutting off his ear.*

48 *Then Jesus said to them, 'Have you come out with swords and clubs to arrest me as though I were a bandit?*

49 *'Day after day I was with you in the temple teaching, and you did not arrest me. But let the scriptures be fulfilled.'*

50 *All of them deserted him and fled.*

51 *A certain young man was following him, wearing nothing but a linen cloth. They caught hold of him,* 52 *but he left the linen cloth and ran off naked.*

Starters

1. *Reflect for a while on the stark contrast between what Judas did externally and his real intentions.*

2. *Contrast the fidelity of Jesus to his mission from the Father and the unfaithfulness of the disciples towards Jesus.*

VII/5. The arrest of Jesus

Jesus is ready and his testing begins at once. Judas, one of the twelve, as Mark repeatedly notes, comes not with disciplined soldiers nor with temple police but with a mob of men armed with knives and clubs. When Judas hands Jesus over to his enemies by a kiss of friendship, Jesus remains silent.

After Judas, the unfaithful disciple, is introduced, no one is named in this present episode except Jesus. It appears that in this manner Mark wants to focus our attention fixedly on the person of Jesus.

When someone makes a show of violence to defend Jesus and cuts off the ear of the high priest's slave, Mark does not directly name this individual as a disciple. Already the disciples are fading from our view. They are mentioned no further in Mark's account of the passion.

The words of Jesus, which Mark records, draw our attention to the infidelity, malice, and violence which surround Jesus at this moment. They do not threaten or accuse anyone, but make clear what is really happening, as God sees things. They point to the trust which Jesus feels towards God, despite the apparent victory of evil and injustice. God foresees the evils that come to his faithful servants as part of the achievement of his divine plan for the world, as scripture makes clear (14:49).

What is the meaning of the young man, whom Mark's Gospel alone mentions? Historically, it is not at all clear who this person may have been. Its symbolic meaning may be more important.

It could be a symbol of Jesus himself as the one who escaped from the shroud of death (15:46) to appear in the shining robe of resurrection (16:5). We may have here an early symbol of Christian faith in Jesus as the one saved by God out of death into the glory of the resurrection.

53 They took Jesus to the high priest; and all the chief priests, the elders and the scribes were assembled. 54 Peter had followed him at a distance, right into the courtyard of the high priest; and he was sitting with the guards, warming himself at the fire.

55 Now the chief priests and the whole council were looking for testimony against Jesus to put him to death; but they found none. 56 For many gave false testimony against him, and their witness did not agree. 57 Some stood up and gave false testimony against him, saying, 58 'We heard him say, "I will destroy this temple that is made with hands, and in three days I will build another, not made with hands." ' 59 But even so on this point their testimony did not agree. 60 And the high priest stood up in the midst, and asked Jesus, 'Have you no answer to make? What is it that these men testify against you?' 61 But he was silent and did not answer. Again the high priest asked him, 'Are you the Messiah, the Son of the Blessed One?' 62 Jesus said, 'I am; "and you will see the Son of Man seated at the right hand of Power," and "coming with the clouds of heaven." '

63 Then the high priest tore his clothes and said, 'Why do we still need witnesses? 64 You have heard his blasphemy! What is your decision?' All of them condemned him as deserving death. 65 Some began to spit on him, to blindfold him, and to strike him, saying to him, 'Prophesy!' The guards also took him over and beat him.

66 While Peter was below in the courtyard, one of the servant-girls of the high priest came by. 67 When she saw Peter warming himself, she stared at him and said, 'You also were with Jesus, the man from Nazareth.' 68 But he denied it, saying, 'I do not know or understand what you are talking about.' And he went out into the forecourt. Then the cock crowed. 69 And the servant-girl, on seeing him, began again to say to the bystanders, 'This man is one of them.' 70 But again he denied it. Then after a little while the bystanders again said to Peter, 'Certainly you are one of them; for you are a Galilean.' 71 But he began to curse, and he swore an oath, 'I do not know this man you are talking about.' 72 At that moment the cock crowed for the second time. Then Peter remembered that Jesus had said to him, 'Before the cock crows twice, you will deny me three times.' And he broke down and wept.

VII/6. The condemnation and denial

Mark consistently focuses attention on Jesus and what really happens to him in the deeper and broader perspectives of God's view of things and how Christian faith quickly came to understand the passion.

Mark is not overly concerned with Jewish legal processes. Nor is his chief aim to give a strict account of historical events. He was unlikely to be in a position to do that, even had he wished. He, like others before him, probably shaped scattered pieces of information about the sufferings of Jesus into the form of a night trial before the Jewish Sanhedrin.

Jesus is before the men of power — priests, elders, and scribes. Peter sits with the servants of the enemies of Jesus, to warm himself in the cold night air of Jerusalem in April. Already we sense the separation of Peter from Jesus, despite his show of loyalty in following him.

The witness against Jesus is false, not because it is necessarily untrue, but because it is given out of malice. The climax comes when the high priest asks Jesus if he is the Messiah and the Son of the Blessed One. For the first time, Jesus clearly accepts these two titles together, Christ and Son of God (1:1).

Standing in weakness before the powers of the land, he is less likely to have his claim to them misunderstood. Yet at once Jesus describes himself as the Messiah in terms of the name he always uses of himself, the Son of Man, but now a Son of Man who will bring the full power of God into the world, in words from a psalm and the prophecy of Daniel (Ps 110:1 and Dan 7:13).

After Jesus is condemned, insults, violence and mockery are heaped upon him by his enemies. Outside, Peter his disciple denies him three times, publicly separating himself from Jesus. Jesus is now entirely alone.

1 As soon as it was morning, the chief priests held a consultation with the elders and scribes and the whole council. They bound Jesus, led him away and handed him over to Pilate.

2 Pilate asked him, 'Are you the King of the Jews?' He answered him, 'You say so.'

3 Then the chief priests accused him of many things.

4 Pilate asked him again, 'Have you no answer? See how many charges they bring against you.'

5 But Jesus made no further reply, so that Pilate was amazed.

6 Now at the festival he used to release a prisoner for them anyone for whom they asked. 7 Now a man called Barabbas was in prison with the rebels who had committed murder during the insurrection. 8 So the crowd came and began to ask Pilate to do for them according to his custom. 9 Then he answered them, 'Do you want me to release for you the King of the Jews?' 10 For he realised that it was out of jealousy that the chief priests had handed him over. 11 But the chief priests stirred up the crowd to have him release Barabbas for them instead. 12 Pilate spoke to them again, 'Then what do you wish me to do with the man whom you call the King of the Jews?' 13 They shouted back, 'Crucify him!' 14 Pilate asked them, 'Why, what evil has he done?' But they shouted all the more, 'Crucify him!'

15 So Pilate, wishing to satisfy the crowd, released Barabbas for them; and after flogging Jesus, he handed him over to be crucified.

Starters

1. *Only in this chapter throughout Mark's Gospel is Jesus named a 'king'. Look up the six times: 15:2, 9, 12, 18, 26, 32.*

2. *Notice how often in Mark's story of the passion Jesus is 'handed over'. Look up the places: 14:10, 11, 18, 21, 41, 42, 44, 15:1, 10, 15.*

VII/7. Jesus is handed over for execution

Now we come to the day of Jesus' death. Early in the morning, the Jewish leaders hand Jesus over to Pilate who is named without any introduction. Mark presumes his readers know who he is.

For the first time the binding of Jesus is mentioned and Jesus is called a king, a political title. This title is used of Jesus by others six times during the last day of his life, yet nowhere else does it appear in Mark's Gospel. Mark seems to suggest the kind of king Jesus really is.

One senses that in reality Jesus is not on trial, but the others — Pilate, the priests, the crowds and Barabbas. The silence of Jesus and his short, probing reply to Pilate show him more as a judge than a defendant. The priests appear to act out of envy towards Jesus.

Pilate, although he recognises that Jesus is not politically dangerous, acts for shallow reasons of political expediency to placate the crowd. The crowd chooses Barabbas, literally 'son of the father,' one who destroys life in others, as the one they want to have among them. The true Son of God, who brings the gospel, they reject and want crucified.

Pilate orders Jesus to be scourged, a usual punishment before crucifixion. It was generally done with leather whips loaded with bone or metal, and the person was sometimes tied to a pillar, perhaps bent over a low pillar.

Then Pilate hands Jesus over to be crucified. This is the tenth time that the phrase has been used by Mark in his story of the passion.

For Christian faith, this can imply a deeper and mysterious handing over of Jesus by God to the world, no matter what the cost, to bring into the world God's power to free from evil and bring life to all.

Mark 15:16-20

16 Then the soldiers led him into the courtyard of the palace (that is, the governor's headquarters); and they called together the whole cohort.

17 And they clothed him in a purple cloak; and after twisting some thorns into a crown, they put it on him.

18 And they began saluting him, 'Hail, King of the Jews!'

19 They struck his head with a reed, spat upon him, and knelt down in homage to him.

20 After mocking him, they stripped him of the purple cloak and put his own clothes on him. Then they led him out to crucify him.

Starters

1. Read this account again slowly and allow the brutality and indignity of the episode to sink into my heart.

2. Reflect prayerfully on the aloneness and weakness of Jesus in this mockery by the mercenaries.

VII/8. Jesus is mocked by the soldiers

The soldiers have heard Jesus called by Pilate the King of the Jews. Three times he has used this title for Jesus (15:2, 9, 12). Now the soldiers, possibly hardened mercenaries from Syria or from some other country unfriendly to the Jews, decide to have their cruel fun with this so-called king of the Jews. It may be their way of giving insult not only to Jesus but to the whole Jewish race, whom they probably despise.

When the soliders take Jesus back to their military barracks, they stage a savage entertainment for themselves by a mock crowning and enthronement. Mark gives stark details of the indignities they inflict on Jesus.

The vivid and detailed description of Mark may even suggest the reports of eye-witnesses and an historical basis for this horrible story of barbaric ridicule and mockery. Jesus, is already weakened and humiliated by the terrible scourging, even before the soliders begin.

The soliders call all their company together to share in the fun. They dress Jesus in a faded purple cloak, probably an old military cloak. They twist some thorns into a rough crown for him. A king must have a crown on his head.

They perhaps seat Jesus somewhere and begin to salute him in mock respect. They call him King of the Jews. Perhaps it is a reed or stick which they have already put into his hands that they use to strike him on the head. Some spit upon him. They kneel before him in mock respect, each one probably trying to outdo the other in cruelty and ridicule. When they have satisfied themselves and finish, they strip the purple cloak from him and dress Jesus in his own clothes again. Jesus will not be led naked through the streets to the place of execution, as it seems those condemned to crucifixion by the Romans commonly were.

21 They compelled a passer-by, who was coming in from the country, to carry his cross; it was Simon of Cyrene, the father of Alexander and Rufus. 22 Then they brought Jesus to the place called Golgotha (which means the place of a skull). 23 And they offered him wine mixed with myrrh; but he did not take it. 24 And they crucified him, and divided his clothes among them, casting lots to decide what each should take. 25 It was nine o'clock in the morning, when they crucified him. 26 The inscription of the charge against him read, 'The King of the Jews.' 27 And with him they crucified two bandits, one on his right and one on his left. 29 Those who passed by derided him, shaking their heads and saying, 'Aha! You who would destroy the temple and build it in three days, 30 save yourself, and come down from the cross!' 31 In the same way the chief priests, along with the scribes, were also mocking him among themselves and saying, 'He saved others; he cannot save himself. 32 Let the Messiah, the King of Israel, come down from the cross now, so that we may see and believe.' Those who were crucified with him also taunted him.

33 When it was noon, darkness came over the whole land until three in the afternoon. 34 At three o'clock Jesus cried out with a loud voice. 'Eloi, Eloi, lama sabach-thani?' which means, 'My God, my God, why have you forsaken me?' 35 When some of the bystanders heard it, they said, 'Listen, he is calling for Elijah.' 36 And someone ran, filled a sponge with sour wine, put it on a stick, and gave it to him to drink, saying, 'Wait, let us see whether Elijah will come to take him down.' 37 Then Jesus gave a loud cry and breathed his last.

38 And the curtain of the temple was torn in two, from top to bottom. 39 Now when the centurion, who stood facing him, saw that in this way he breathed his last, he said, 'Truly this man was God's Son!'

40 There were also women looking on from a distance; among them were Mary Magdalene, and Mary the mother of James the younger and of Joses, and Salome. 41 These used to follow him and provided for him when he was in Galilee; and there were many other women who came up with him to Jerusalem.

VII/9. The crucifixion of Jesus

The death of Jesus is the final climax of his revelation to the world of the power of God. With the identification of Jesus as the Son of God by God himself at the river and on the mountain, by himself in his passion (14:62), and now by a Gentile at the cross (15:39), the four great 'pillars' of Mark's Gospel are in place.

In the journey to Golgotha, about 500 metres, a stranger forced to carry the cross after Jesus emphasises his aloneness. The crucifying begins about nine in the morning.

A humanitarian offering of wine, drugged with myrrh to reduce pain, is made, but Jesus refuses it. He hangs naked on the cross, for his clothes are divided among his executioners. He is called a king in the charge against him put above his head, as he hangs on a cross between the two bandits.

The two bandits, the passers-by, the priests, and the scribes mock Jesus as one who can destroy the temple and rebuild it in three days and who saves others but not himself. They taunt him to do what he cannot do — to be a king without the cross. The truth is spoken in the malice and blindness of those who speak it.

The darkness at midday aptly symbolises how none see what is really happening. At three, when Jesus calls out, someone from compassion, or curiosity to see if Elijah will come, offers him vinegar. But Jesus with a cry of strength breathes out his life.

The tearing open of the temple veil dramatically symbolises that the power of God is no longer separated and hidden from the world, but is made accessible to all through the death of Jesus. The centurion before Jesus, proclaims him Son of God at a time he appears hardly human, while the faithful women from Galilee watch everything from a distance.

42 When evening had come, and since it was the day of Preparation, that is, the day before the sabbath, 43 Joseph of Arimathea, a respected member of the council, who was also himself waiting expectantly for the kingdom of God, went boldly to Pilate and asked for the body of Jesus.

44 Then Pilate wondered if he were already dead; and summoning the centurion, he asked him whether he had been dead for some time.

45 When he learned from the centurion that he was dead, he granted the body to Joseph.

46 Then Joseph bought a linen cloth, and taking down the body, wrapped it in the linen cloth, and laid it in a tomb which had been hewn out of the rock. He then rolled a stone against the door of the tomb.

47 Mary Magdalene and Mary the mother of Joses saw where he was laid.

Starters

1. Consider the signs of the poverty in which Jesus died.

2. Place myself with the women from Galilee and let me try to share their feelings as they watched the burial of Jesus by others.

VII/10. The burial of Jesus

It was apparently a Roman practice to let bodies rot on their crosses or be eaten by wild animals. For pious Jews, to whom death was incomplete without burial and who lived according to the law as it was interpreted by the Book of Deuteronomy (Deut 21:22-23), this was unthinkable.

A prominent member of the Jewish Sanhedrin, Joseph from Arimathaea, the location of which is unknown, comes forward to perform this last act of piety for the dead Jesus.

Since Joseph is not a disciple of Jesus, Mark again draws attention to the desertion of Jesus by all his disciples. He was waiting expectantly, Mark notes, for the coming of the kingdom of God, suggesting it is more than Jewish piety or respect for the law that inspires him to go courageously to Pilate and ask for the body of Jesus who faithfully proclaimed the coming of the kingdom of God.

The truth that Jesus really died on the cross, against some early doubters, is reinforced by the action attributed to Pilate. He calls the centurion who was in charge of the execution to verify from him that Jesus is truly dead.

The devotion and care of Joseph, the non-disciple, is detailed for us in several ways. He buys a piece of fine linen as a shroud for the corpse of Jesus. He provides a tomb cut from rock. He rolls a stone, no doubt with the help of servants, across the entrance of the tomb. These devout actions of Joseph also highlight the extreme poverty in which Jesus dies.

The faithful women stand silently watching all that Joseph does and where he hastily buries the body of Jesus, because it is already evening and the Sabbath rest begins at sunset. The women see that the corpse of Jesus is buried without the customary anointing of ointments and spices.

Mark 16:1-8

1 When the sabbath was over, Mary Magdalene, and Mary the mother of James, and Salome bought spices, so that they might go and anoint him.

2 And very early on the first day of the week, when the sun had risen, they went to the tomb.

3 They had been saying to one another, 'Who will roll away the stone for us from the entrance to the tomb?'

4 When they looked up, they saw that the stone, which was very large, had already been rolled back.

5 As they entered the tomb, they saw a young man, dressed in a white robe, sitting on the right side; and they were alarmed.

6 But he said to them, 'Do not be alarmed; you are looking for Jesus of Nazareth, who was crucified. He has been raised; he is not here. Look, there is the place they laid him.

7 'But go, tell his disciples and Peter that he is going ahead of you to Galilee; there you will see him, just as he told you.'

8 So they went out and fled from the tomb, for terror and amazement had seized them; and they said nothing to anyone, for they were afraid.

Starters

1. *Reflect on how the gospel of Christ's resurrection is first announced here to those who have remained faithful.*

2. *Reflect on the situation: the darkness of the tomb becoming light, silence the word of God, and emptiness and newness of life.*

VII/11. The women find an empty tomb

As the passion story began with a woman at Bethany anointing Jesus (14:3-9), so now it ends with the women coming to anoint his body in the tomb. The faithfulness of women 'frames' the unfaithfulness of men.

The women, the only ones who have not deserted Jesus, go early to the tomb and find it empty. The sun, already risen, can also be a symbol of Jesus already risen. The young man, as in Gethsemani (14:51-52), suggests Jesus, now risen and at the right-hand of God, sharing the fulness of divine power. Does his message mean that Jesus may first have revealed his resurrection in a veiled manner to the faithful women through the unlikely sign of a dark, silent and empty tomb?

Galilee, where the disciples are told to go, was the place of beginnings, the place where Jesus first called his disciples and challenged them in astonishment and terror with the gospel of the kingdom of God. Now they are to go there to see the gospel of the raising by God of the crucified Jesus.

The strange ending to Mark's Gospel puzzled Christians from the earliest times, it seems, since other endings were soon added. Most today, however, favour verse 8 as the original ending. If what Mark intended to write was the 'beginning' of the gospel of Jesus as the Christ and Son of God (1:1), it makes sense that he concludes before the resurrection of Jesus is recognised by his disciples. The shocked and terrified women become a symbol of the moment before the gospel of resurrection bursts upon the world, but they too, like the disciples, become unfaithful by saying nothing.

Luke portrayed the beginnings of the mystery of the incarnation of Jesus by a frightened, obedient woman (Lk 1:29-30), but Mark presents the beginnings of the mystery of the resurrection of Jesus by frightened, disobedient women (16:8).

⁹*Now when he rose early on the first day of the week, he appeared first to Mary Magdalene, from whom he had cast out seven demons.* ¹⁰*She went out and told those who had been with him, while they were mourning and weeping.* ¹¹*But when they heard that he was alive and had been seen by her, they would not believe it.*

¹²*After this he appeared in another form to two of them, as they were walking into the country.* ¹³*And they went back and told the rest, but they did not believe them.*

¹⁴*Later he appeared to the eleven themselves as they were sitting at the table; and he upbraided them for their lack of faith and stubbornness, because they had not believed those who saw him after he had risen.* ¹⁵*And he said to them, 'Go into all the world and proclaim the good news to the whole creation.* ¹⁶*The one who believes and is baptised will be saved; but the one who does not believe will be condemned.*

¹⁷*And these signs will accompany those who believe: by using my name they will cast out demons; they will speak in new tongues;* ¹⁸*they will pick up snakes in their hands, and if they drink any deadly thing, it will not hurt them; they will lay their hands on the sick, and they will recover.'*

¹⁹*So then the Lord Jesus, after he had spoken to them, was taken up into heaven and sat down at the right hand of God.* ²⁰*And they went out and proclaimed the good news everywhere, while the Lord worked with them and confirmed the message by the signs that accompanied it.*

The shorter ending of Mark

And all that had been commanded them they told briefly to those around Peter. And afterwards Jesus himself sent out through them, from east to west, the sacred and imperishable proclamation of eternal salvation.

Appendix: Appearances of the risen Christ

The appendix to Mark's Gospel, or its 'Longer Ending', to distinguish it from a shorter ending also added later, was probably written in the second century by an author with a markedly different literary style from the original author of the early seventies.

The Christian community wanted descriptions of appearances of the risen Jesus, as in the three other Gospels, and this ending to Mark's Gospel eventually became generally accepted along with the rest of his Gospel.

The appendix has four sections which appear to be short summaries of the appearances of the risen Jesus which are described in the other three Gospels and the Acts of the Apostles.

The appearance of Jesus to Mary Magdalene (9-11) summarises what is in Matthew (28:9-10) and in John (20:1-2, 11-18).

The appearance to the two travellers (12-13) summarises what is in Luke (24:13-35).

The appearance of Jesus to the Eleven at table, to whom he gave a mission to announce the gospel of his resurrection (14-18), summarises what is in Matthew (28:16-20), in Luke (24:36-49 and Acts 1:6-8) and in John (20:19-23).

The taking of Jesus into heaven and the proclamation of the gospel by the disciples (19-20) summarises what is found in Luke (24:50-53 and Acts 1:9-11 and the rest of Acts).

In a 'Shorter Ending', the women tell Peter and those with him, what they heard, and Jesus sends out the message of salvation through the disciples.

FURTHER READING

I have found the following books especially insightful, and I recommend them to others for further help in exploring the riches of the Gospel according to Mark:

MARK, Wilfrid Harrington, OP, Dublin: Veritas Publications, 1984 (1979).

MARK'S STORY OF JESUS, Werner H. Kelber, Philadelphia: Fortress Press, 1988 (1979).

THE CALL TO DISCIPLESHIP, David Stanley, SJ, London: The Way Supplement 43/44, 1982.

THE MESSAGE OF MARK, Morna D. Hooker, London: Epworth Press, 1983.

Printed and bound in Australia by
Southwood Press Pty Limited, Marrickville, 2204